ENFORCEMENT IN THE MAGISTRATES' COURT

by

Steven Reynolds
LLB, MBA, DipM, MCIM, Barrister

and

Ian Lomax
LLB, MSocSc, FIMgt, MIPD, Barrister

CLT PROFESSIONAL PUBLISHING
A DIVISION OF CENTRAL LAW TRAINING LTD

Published by
CLT Professional Publishing
A Division of Central Law Training Ltd
Wrens Court
52–54 Victoria Road
Sutton Coldfield
Birmingham
B72 1SX

ISBN 1 85811 095 5

Typeset by Adrian McLaughlin
Printed in Great Britain by Redwood Books, Trowbridge, Wiltshire

Contents

3. Non-Custodial Enforcement Measures

4. Imprisonment and Detention for Non-Payment of Fines

PART 6 ATTACHMENT OF EARNINGS

Preface

Imprisonment for debt in England and Wales was abolished by Parliament in 1869. Despite this our prisons contain, at any one time, thousands of people who have been imprisoned for failure to pay a sum of money. The reason for this apparent contradiction is that whilst the Debtors Act abolished imprisonment for debt in general, it expressly retained it for a number of classes of default, namely fines, maintenance, rates and certain instances of civil debt where monies are owed to the Exchequer.

In the context of the overall (and currently rising) prison population the daily intake of debtors is small and the lengths of commitment equally short. Nevertheless, the issue has become one of some social importance with a continued diet of documentaries, books and newspaper articles being fed to the public regarding the injustice of it all – the point being that these people may have reached prison not because they have committed offences for which the court would or could have imposed imprisonment as a fitting penalty, but because their failure to comply with a monetary order of the court.

Not surprisingly, the system has its critics and there are many who argue that in its effect upon a person's character, the suffering caused to family and dependents, the interruption of work, and the possibility of failing to find work upon release, the use of imprisonment is often out of all proportion to the wrong which has been committed, or the default. Others argue with equal vigour that imprisonment must be retained as the ultimate sanction and cannot be dispensed with if the integrity of the rule of law and the credibility of the courts' monetary orders are to be maintained.

These arguments are set to run and run. It is not the purpose of this book to debate the argument but simply to explain the workings of the law as regards enforcement in the magistrates' court. Quite evidently, the courts are able, by the use of alternative powers, to deal effectively with the vast majority of defaulters who never go within a mile of the prison gates. It is these alternative powers with which the book is equally concerned. Only by fully understanding the alternatives to custody can a court ensure that when imprisonment is imposed, all other available options have been tried or at least considered and rejected for valid and lawful reasons. Failure to do so will be a constant 'achilles heel' to the magistrates' courts as clearly indicated by Simon Brown LJ in *Cawley* when he stated:

"Offenders generally and young offenders in particular ought not to be locked up for non-payment of fines unless no sensible alternative presents itself. Down the years too many have been. Time and again committees have voiced this view and time and again Parliament has legislated to promote it. Much of the legislation is directed at magistrates' courts and it includes provisions requiring various matters to be specified in the warrant of commitment if commitment there must be. The ... lawfulness of the approach to committing fine defaulters in many magistrates' courts, is ... now threatening to overload the facilities of this court ... If justices are properly fastidious as to when to commit, and reason their decisions and complete their warrants as this judgement indicates is required, the present problem will resolve itself. Otherwise this court will be engulfed. The message is clear."

This book has had a number of re-incarnations since the mid-1980s and we have continued to be heartened by two events. The first is the books durability as a working guide within offices, despite some radical changes in the law (e.g. Child Support Act, Community Charge, Council Tax etc.) along the way. The second is the wide acceptance given to the book by a number of diverse organisations connected in some way with the enforcement process. If the mid-1990's have seen one major change in this area, it is the increasing interest shown by private law firms to the area of fine enforcement. In some instances the increasing availability of legal aid has been the motivating factor; in others it has provided an opportunity for reputations to be made. A word of warning may be appropriate here. Both authors have worked in the area of enforcement for many years. It has always been a "Cinderella" subject relative to other legal subjects; and will remain a "Cinderella" subject in the future. The enforcement of fines, maintenance etc. is a hard business and getting harder by the year. It is an area of the law which requires pragmatism, common sense and realism; rich pickings, politics (with a small 'p') and ideology are best left out of the equation.

We have taken, once again, the opportunity not only to bring all the chapters up to date, but also, with the benefit of hindsight or different perception, to handle the subject matter in a different way.

Finally, our thanks go to those who have greatly assisted in the preparation of the text. They are Debbie Scott (Manchester) and Sally Veasey (Exeter) for their secretarial and administrative support; and to

Dawn Windsor-Bush (Manchester) and Valerie Cave (Exeter) for their legal input and contribution to the text. Any errors and omissions, however, remain our exclusive responsibility.

Steven Reynolds
Ian Lomax
March 1996

Acknowledgements
The forms in Appendix 2 are Crown copyright and are reproduced with the permission of the Controller of HMSO.

Table of Cases

Table of Statutes, Practice Directions and Circulars

Practice Directions

Circulars

Table of Statutory Instruments

PART I: ENFORCEMENT OF FINES, COSTS AND COMPENSATION

CHAPTER 1

Initial Enforcement Activity

CHAPTER 1

Initial Enforcement Activity

Introduction

Generally fines, costs, compensation and forfeited recognisances are all recovered in the same way (Magistrates' Court Act (MCA) 1980, ss 150(1)(3) and 120(4)).

A fine is generally regarded and defined by statute as a monetary penalty imposed by a magistrates' court on the conviction of an individual for an offence. However a fine is not the only kind of monetary payment which may be ordered at the time of a conviction. A person may also be ordered to pay costs and possibly compensation, but these other payments are not necessarily "fines" in the strict sense. Nevertheless for most purposes they are recovered in the same way as fines with some important differences; however for most purposes it can be said that the different forms of monetary payments ordered at the time of a conviction, whatever they may be, can be recovered as if each was a fine. This also applies to forfeited recognisances.

All the enforcement steps which are set out in the text can be treated as applying generally to all the forms of monetary payments ordered at the time of a conviction; where there are differences this is explained in the text.

It is therefore possible to use the word "fine" as a generic term to refer to all the different types of payment which can be ordered at the time of a conviction. However caution is sometimes required because there are occasions when "fine" is used in a narrow sense to refer only to the pecuniary penalty imposed for the offence.

Fixing the amount of the fine

Before going on to consider the various methods of recovery of fines, without doubt the first step towards effective enforcement must be by the court fixing of the fine at a level appropriate to the offender's means.

Before fixing the amount of any fine the court must inquire into an offender's financial circumstances. The amount of the fine must be such as, in the court's opinion, reflects the seriousness of the offence and takes into account the offender's financial circumstances.

In cases where an offender has been convicted in his absence or has not provided the court with a statement of his means or does not provide the information orally, then the court may make such determination as to the offender's means as it thinks fit (Criminal Justice Act (CJA) 1991, s 18).

It used to be generally thought that any fine imposed by the court should be capable of repayment within a 12-month period from the date of the conviction; however this is no longer the case. In *R* v *Olliver and Olliver* (1989) 153 JP 369, it was said that there was nothing wrong in principle in ordering the period of repayment for fines and other amounts by instalments to extend over a period of two or even three years, provided this did not place an undue burden on an offender and was not at the same time too severe a punishment, having regard to the nature of the offence and the offender. It was said that if the fine or compensation was within the offender's capacity to pay over a period of two or three years, in such a way that default and any subsequent penalty was unlikely, then in an appropriate case, there was no reason why this course should not be taken. However what the case does not say is that a two- or three-year period is to be regarded as a general rule or norm. It would appear that before a court makes an order for payment extending over a two- or three-year period there is a need for caution. The circumstances must be such that it is proper for the payment to be made over such a period so that no undue burden is placed on an offender and default must be seen to be unlikely.

Where fines are set at a level which is too high for an offender, recovery becomes difficult. Payments which extend over long periods almost invariably lead to default. Perhaps the former law which suggested a 12-month period as being appropriate could still be followed, with exceptions being made under the principles set out in *Olliver*.

In summary when fixing the amount of a fine a court should:

- take account of an offender's means; and
- fix the fine at a level which allows an offender to clear the fine generally within a year, exceptionally two to three years.

Order for statement of offenders' means

It may be that circumstances arise when a court does not have information about an offender's financial circumstances. Here the court can, before sentencing, make a financial circumstances order. This requires an individual to give to the court within a period specified by the court, such a statement of his financial circumstances as the court may require. There is a complete discretion vested in the court. It is open to the court to specify precisely the financial information it requires (CJA 1991, s 20).

An order can be made at any time after an offender has been convicted of an offence but before he has been sentenced. It can be made even where the court has information of an offender's financial circumstances but is not satisfied with the information that is being given.

Where a case is proceeding by way of the guilty plea by post procedure (MCA 1980, s 12(4)) an order can also be made where the court is notified that an individual desires to plead guilty without appearing before the court. This means that an order can be made before a conviction if appropriate, in this one circumstance.

It is an offence to fail without reasonable excuse to comply with a financial circumstances order rendering an offender liable on summary conviction to a fine not exceeding £1,000.

It is also an offence when furnishing a statement in compliance with an order to make a statement which is known to be false or to make a reckless statement which is false, or knowingly fail to disclose any material fact. Here the penalty on summary conviction is imprisonment for a term not exceeding three months or a fine not exceeding £2,500 or both.

Official request for statement as to financial circumstances

Although a financial circumstances order can usually only be made after a person has been convicted of an offence, it is open to the magistrates' court clerk prior to a conviction to request an individual to provide a statement of financial circumstances for the purpose of informing the court, in the event of his being convicted, of his finances in determining the amount of any fine. Making such a request can save time and can avoid the need for a financial circumstances order.

Although there is no penalty for failure to comply with a request to provide such information, it is an offence for an individual in response to such a request to make a statement which he knows to be false, or to recklessly furnish a statement which is false, or to knowingly fail to disclose any material fact. The penalty on summary conviction of such an offence is imprisonment for a term not exceeding three months or a fine not exceeding £2,500 or both (CJA 1991, s 20A).

Time to pay and payment by instalments

Where an offender is ordered to pay a sum on conviction for an offence, the court may require immediate repayment, allow time for payment, or order payments by instalments (MCA 1980, s 75).

Where time for payment has been allowed as distinguished from payments by instalments, a court or justices' clerk (or a designated member of his staff) may on application by or on behalf of the person liable to make the payments, allow further time to pay or order payments by instalments (MCA 1980, s 75(2); Justices' Clerks Rules 1970, Sched, paras 6, 6A). Application for time to pay must be made in writing. The applicant need not attend the hearing unless the court so requires (Magistrates' Courts Rules 1981, r 51).

The application does not have to be made by the person liable to make payment, but may instead be made on his behalf by, for example, parents, husbands and wives, probation officers or solicitors.

Where the court originally ordered payment by instalments it may, on application of the person liable to pay the outstanding sum, vary the number of instalments payable, the amount of any instalments payable and the date on which any instalment becomes payable (MCA 1980, s 85A). In this circumstance the application must be made by the person liable to make payment and not by a person acting on his behalf.

Where payment by instalments has been ordered it often occurs that an individual misses a payment only to bring himself up to date at a later stage. In these circumstances where any default is made then the total amount outstanding may be enforced. This means that should an individual miss only one payment, then whether or not he later brings himself up to date with payments he is treated as having defaulted in paying all the outstanding instalments and the full balance outstanding can be enforced (MCA 1980, s 75(3)).

Requiring offender to return to court at later date

Where a court allows time to pay or orders payment by instalments, it may at its discretion fix a date when the offender must return to court under section 86 of the MCA 1980 if at that date,

1. where instalment payments have been allowed, any instalment falling due remains unpaid; or
2. where time for payment has been allowed, and any part of the original sum remains unpaid.

The purpose of the defendant's return to court for an inquiry to be made into his means and the reasons for non-payment. At such a hearing the court may consider issuing a warrant committing the defendant to prison, subject to the restrictions on imposing imprisonment in default of payment. Although imprisonment may ultimately be imposed for failure to pay a fine, the power to impose imprisonment may only be exercised after an inquiry into the defendant's means, subject to limited exceptions (see pxx below). An attendance at court at a hearing fixed in advance as above qualifies as a means inquiry for this purpose.

At the hearing the court may if it wishes allow further time to pay or vary the rate of payments, if appropriate, without resorting to other methods of enforcement.

The power to fix in advance a date upon which the offender is to return to court is one which may be exercised at the time of convicting the offender or at a later date, but only in each case in the offender's presence (MCA 1980, s 86(2)).

It is also open to the court to fix a later date in substitution for the date originally fixed (MCA 1980, s 86(3)). The power to substitute another day for the day originally fixed may be exercised by a single justice or by the justices' clerk (Justices' Clerks Rules 1970, Sched, para 17). Notice in writing of the substituted day must be served on the offender. Service may be effected in the same way in which service of a summons may be effected (Magistrates' Courts Rules 1981, r 52). The substitution of a date for that originally fixed may be done in the offender's absence.

Should an offender fail to appear in person on a day fixed for his return to court under either of the above provisions and, where time to pay has been allowed any part of the summary remains unpaid or, where instalments have been allowed, any instalment which has fallen due remains unpaid, the court may issue a warrant to bring the offender before the court. However, note that where a day has been fixed in the offender's absence in substitution for a day previously fixed, a warrant on his arrest on a failure to appear may not be issued unless it is proved to the court, on oath, or in such manner as may be prescribed, that notice in writing of the substituted day was served on the offender in what appears to the court to be a reasonable time before that day.

Imprisonment at the time of conviction

Although imprisonment in default of payment is looked at in detail later in the book, it is as well to consider imprisonment briefly at this stage because at the time of convicting an offender it is possible for the court to impose imprisonment. The power to impose imprisonment in default of payment of a fine applies equally to costs, compensation and forfeited recognisances.

Where a court convicts an offender and orders him to pay a fine, costs or compensation or forfeits of recognisance, the court may impose imprisonment at the same time where

1. in the case of an offence punishable by imprisonment (this excludes forfeited recognisances: see MCA 1980, s 120(4)) the offender appears to the court to have sufficient means to pay the sum forthwith or
2. it appears that the offender is likely to remain long enough at a place of abode in the United Kingdom to enable payment of the sum to be enforced by other methods or
3. on the occasion of the conviction the court sentences the offender to immediate imprisonment, detention in a young offender institution or, where the offender is already serving a sentence of custody for life, a term of imprisonment, detention in a young offender institution or in the case of an offender under 21 years of age detention in default of payment of other sums.

Should imprisonment be imposed the court may issue the warrant of commitment forthwith or instead postpone the issue of the warrant.

The restrictions on imposing imprisonment on an occasion after the occasion of convicting an offender does not apply where imprisonment is imposed at the time of conviction. These provisions are set out on page xx).

Note that imprisonment cannot be imposed on an offender unless he is over 20 years of age. The position for persons under this age are set out on page xx.

The notice of penalty

Where the court orders an offender to pay a fine, costs or compensation or orders a recognisance to be forfeited and:

- the court allows time for payment;
- the court directs payment by instalments; or
- the offender is absent when the sum is imposed,

enforcement proceedings cannot be brought for default in payment until the court clerk has served on the offender a notice in writing stating the amount of the sum imposed and, if it is to be paid by instalments, the amount of the instalments, the date on which the sum of each instalment is to be paid, and the place and times at which payment may be made (Magistrates' Courts Rules 1981, r 46). This requirement also applies where a magistrates' court is required to enforce a fine imposed or recognisance forfeited by the Crown Court.

The notice is to be served by delivering it to the offender or by sending it to him by post in a letter addressed to him at his last known or usual place of abode. Form 46 of the Magistrates' Courts (Forms) Rules 1981 is the prescribed form of notice.

Recording details of enforcement

Whenever enforcement proceedings are taken an entry must be made in the court register, or any separate record kept for the purpose of any of the following enforcement steps under rule 65(1)(2)of the Magistrates' Court Rules 1981:

1. Where a court on the occasion of convicting an offender of an offence issues a warrant of commitment for defaulting paying a fine or sum treated as such or, where the court fixes a term of imprisonment at the time of conviction that postpones the issue of the warrant, the reasons for the court's decision.

2. The particulars of any:

(a) means inquiry;
(b) hearing with a view to the issue of a Commitment Warrant;
(c) allowance of further time to pay;
(d) direction to pay by instalments or any variation thereof;
(e) distress for enforcement;
(f) attachment of earnings;
(g) making of a money payment supervision order;
(h) order remitting the whole or part of any fine;
(i) order remitting the whole or part of any forfeited recognisance;
(j) giving of authority for the taking of proceedings in the High Court or county court for the recovery of the sum outstanding;
(k) making of a transfer of fine order;
(l) order transferring the fine to the court;
(m) order made by the Crown Court which specifies the court as the appropriate court to enforce a fine imposed or recognisance forfeited by the Crown Court;

(n) fine imposed or recognisance forfeited by a coroner that has to be treated as having been imposed or forfeited by the court;
(o) reference to the court by a Justice of the Peace of an application to review the terms on which a warrant of commitment is postponed;
(p) order varying the time for which all the conditions subject to which a warrant of commitment is postponed.

CHAPTER 2

Jurisdiction

CHAPTER 2

Jurisdiction

Introduction

Issues of jurisdiction can often arise as part of the enforcement process. The magistrates' court has jurisdiction not only to recover fines which it has imposed, but may also have jurisdiction to recover fines imposed by the Crown Court, other magistrates' court and other bodies.

Jurisdiction is also given to the magistrates' court clerk, in certain circumstances, to take proceedings in the High Court or county court for the recovery of fines. With regard to companies jurisdiction is given to allow the magistrates' court clerk to take civil proceedings to recover outstanding fines.

Territorial jurisdiction is sometimes an issue, as are the powers now available to allow civilian enforcement officers to execute warrants of arrest and warrants of commitment with regard to outstanding fines.

Channel Islands and the Isle of Man

To date the various statutory enforcement provisions concerning recovery of fines which are available in England and Wales, Scotland and Northern Ireland have not generally been extended to the Channel Islands or the Isle of Man, which do not form part of the United Kingdom. This means that where a person lives in either the Channel Islands or the Isle of Man enforcement steps cannot be taken against that person. Perhaps where a person resides in one of these jurisdictions, it would mean that at the time of conviction a court could consider imprisonment in default of payment because the individual is not resident at a place in the United Kingdom.

Note that it is possible to execute a distress warrant in the Isle of Man by virtue of the Summary Jurisdiction Process (Isle of Man) Order 1928. However service of notice of a hearing at which a distress warrant is to be issued could make even this provision difficult to apply.

Transfer of fine orders

Where a magistrates' court is responsible for recovering a fine, and it becomes apparent that the person liable to pay lives outside the court's geographical jurisdiction, a transfer of fine order can be made which transfers responsibility for recovery to another magistrates' court. The order can be made in respect of fines, costs, compensation and forfeited recognisances. The geographical jurisdiction of the magistrates' court is confined to the petty sessions area for which it is responsible.

1. England and Wales

Where it appears to the convicting court that a defendant resides within the area of another magistrates' court, the convicting court (or justices' clerk) may make a transfer of fine order making payment enforceable by the other court. The effect is to transfer from one court to another all functions relating to the collection and enforcement of the sum outstanding. However, for persons aged under 18, not all functions are transferred. It is not possible to transfer the power to make an order requiring a parent or guardian of a youth to enter a recognisance to ensure that the sum outstanding is paid or the power to order that a parent or guardian pay an outstanding sum instead of being paid by the youth. These powers are specifically excluded from transfer (MCA 1980, s 89(1), (2) and (4)).

Once made there is no mechanism by which a transfer of fine order can be revoked or 'withdrawn' even though it may later turn out that the defendant has never even lived in the area of the court of transfer. All that is required to give jurisdiction for the making of the order is that it should appear to the transferring court that the person concerned 'resides' in the area of the other court. The court of transfer should not return the order to the original court because a view is taken that the defendant does not live within that court's area. However if it appears to the court of transfer that the offender is residing within the area of another court, a further transfer of fine order can be made (MCA 1980, s 89(3)). Form 59 of the Magistrates' Courts (Forms) Rules 1981 is the prescribed form of order.

The words of section 89 of the MCA 1980, which empower courts to make transfer of fine orders, are clear and unambiguous and are not subject to any limitation or restriction upon transfer "only in certain circumstance". Thus it is argued that a transfer of fine order can be made even where a person liable to make payments has been committed to prison in default of payment and the issue of the warrant of commitment has been postponed (see page xx); the court of transfer, in the event of default in the terms of the postponement, then has power to carry out the function that the court of transfer would have had — to issue the warrant of commitment. This is a function transferred under the order. The wording of the statute itself would appear to override any difficulty which might otherwise seem to arise where one court imposes imprisonment, postpones the issue of the warrant and then at a later date another court issues the warrant. The function of issuing the warrant is transferred under the order and this would seem clear from the statute's wording. It is also submitted that the contents of section 77 of the 1980 Act, which permits courts to reconsider the terms of postponed commitments makes it essential that courts should be able to transfer fines and other sums where imprisonment has been imposed and the issue of the warrant postponed. It may be that a defendant is living some distance from the original court once the warrant of commitment falls to be issued. In such a case it is in his interest that he should be able to appear before a court to show the court why the warrant should not be issued. The person liable to make payment will be in a much better position to attend court if the court is local. It may be that there is considerable force in the argument that where a defendant subject to a postponed commitment has moved to another area and the warrant falls to be issued, then not only can the fine be transferred but that it should be!

Furthermore, section 72A of the Magistrates' Courts Act 1952, now repealed and replaced by section 90 of the 1980 Act, formally provided that a transfer of fine order to Scotland could be made except when a term of imprisonment had been fixed. Here a clear restriction on the power to transfer was included in the statutory provision. By contrast, section 72 of the 1952 Act, concerning transfers within England and Wales, contained no such restriction. If it is to be said that nevertheless the effect in each case was the same, then the words of prohibition in the one case were at the very least superfluous. It is submitted that this was not the intention of Parliament and that the words were not superfluous, but were there for a purpose. A difference between the two situations was clearly intended to exist and did exist. In one case a transfer of fine order could be made after imprisonment had been fixed but in the other it could not, and sense is made of the statutory provisions.

Although the 1952 Act has been repealed, section 89 of the 1980 Act replaces the former provision and save for one exception is identical. The effect, it is submitted, is as before. It is interesting to note that section 90 of the MCA 1980, which deals with transfers to Scotland and Northern Ireland, no longer contains any words of prohibition. The absence of words of prohibition fell to be considered by the High Court in *R* v *Avon*

Magistrates' Courts Committee, ex parte Bath Law Society (1987) 151 JP 825. Here it was held that, although there had been some doubt in the past whether a court could remand a defendant to any court in a county, as there was nothing in the MCA 1980 to prevent a justice from doing so, the practice was therefore lawful. While this is not direct authority for transfer of fine orders, it is a case where, in the absence of words of prohibition, the High Court ruled that an action could be taken. By analogy the same principle could be applied to a transfer of fine order.

The provisions concerning transfer of fine orders do not apply to legal aid contribution orders, for which separate statutory provision is made with regard to their transfer.

2. Scotland and Northern Ireland

Where it appears to a magistrates' court that the person liable to pay is residing in the area of a court of summary jurisdiction in Scotland, or within any petty sessions district in Northern Ireland, the magistrates' court may order that payment of the sum outstanding shall be enforced by the court in Scotland or Northern Ireland acting for the area in which the person then resides (MCA 1980, s 90). A court may make an order even though a term of imprisonment in default of payment has been imposed and the issue of the commitment warrant postponed (see above).

The order must specify the court of summary jurisdiction by which or petty sessions district in which the payment of the sum is to be enforced. Where payment is to be enforced in Scotland, and the sum involved is more than £100 or is a fine imposed by the Crown Court or the Sheriff Court, the court to be specified in the order must be the sheriff court and not a district court (MCA 1980, s 90(2)).

From the date of the making of the order all functions that relate to satisfaction and enforcement which would have been exercisable by the court making the order will cease. The power to make orders against parents or guardians of persons aged under 18 years, in the same way as transfer of fine orders within England and Wales, cannot be transferred.

In the case of a transfer from Scotland or Northern Ireland under which payment is to be enforced in a magistrates' court in England and Wales, the court specified in the order as the responsible court for enforcement will have all functions it would have had had the sum transferred been imposed by that court and as if any order made in relation to the sum before the transfer of fine order had also been made by that court (MCA 1980, s 91(1)). Again, however, there is no power to make orders against parents and guardians of persons aged under 18.

Where a transfer of fine order has been made under section 403 of the Criminal Procedure (Scotland) Act 1975, or section 104A of the Magistrates' Courts (Northern Ireland) Act 1964 which in either case transfers enforcement to a magistrates' court in England and Wales, that court will have all the like functions as if it were a magistrates' court by which payment of the fine fell to be enforced under an order made by virtue of section 32(1) of the Powers of Criminal Courts Act 1973 (PCCA) (enforcement of Crown Court fines), and as if any order made in respect of the fine before the transfer had been made by that magistrates' court. Again, however, this does not include the power to make orders against parents and guardians of persons aged under 18 years.

Form 60 of the Magistrates' Courts (Forms) Rules 1981 is the prescribed form of order for transfers to Scotland or Northern Ireland.

Procedure

The court clerk making a transfer of fine order in England and Wales is required to send to the court of transfer a copy of the order. Where the fine was originally ordered to be paid by a court in Scotland or Northern Ireland and a magistrates' court makes a transfer of fine order, the magistrates' court clerk on transfer must send a copy of the order to the Scottish court clerk or the Northern Ireland Court clerk which imposed the fine originally.

Where the Magistrates' Court clerk receives a transfer of fine order, whether made in England, Wales, Scotland or Northern Ireland, he is required to deliver or send by post to the offender notice in writing in the prescribed form (Form 61 of the Magistrates' Court (Forms) Rules 1981).

Any money collected under a transfer of fine order is dealt with as if the collecting court had imposed the fine, except where a fine is transferred to a court in England and Wales from a court in Scotland or Northern Ireland. In this case the money is not applied as follows (Magistrates' Courts Rules 1981, r 57(4)):

(i) if the sum is paid, the court clerk receiving payment is required to send the money received to the court clerk in Scotland or Northern Ireland; or

(ii) if the sum is not paid the clerk of the collecting court is required to inform the court clerk in Scotland or Northern Ireland of the manner in which the adjudication has been satisfied, or that the sum or any balance thereof appears to be irrecoverable.

Crown Court fines

Where a fine is imposed or recognisance forfeited by the Crown Court, the sum payable is recovered in a magistrates' court and is treated for collection, enforcement and remission purposes as having been imposed or forfeited by the magistrates' court specified in the order made by the Crown Court or, if no such order is made, the magistrates' court by whom the offender was committed to the Crown Court to be tried or otherwise dealt with (PCCA 1973, s 32(1)).

Note however that a magistrates' court cannot remit a Crown Court fine or recognisance forfeited by the Crown Court without first obtaining the Crown Court's consent (PCCA 1973, s 32(4)).

On imposing a fine, the Crown Court may allow time for payment or order payment by instalments (PCCA 1973, s 31(1)). The power to allow time for payment or to order payment by instalments also applies to costs and compensation ordered by the Crown Court (PCCA 1973, s 34).

Where the Crown Court imposes a fine or forfeits a recognisance, it must also make an order fixing a term of imprisonment (or detention in default of payment for offenders between the ages of 18 and 20) which is to be served in the event that the sum is not duly paid. In the event of default, where the court considers imprisonment or detention it is the period prescribed by the Crown Court, less any deduction for part payment, which is the period to be contained in any commitment warrant (see further p xx) (PCCA 1973, s 31). Note that the Crown Court does not have power to impose imprisonment or detention in default for non-payment of costs or compensation *(R* v *Komsta and Murphy* (1990) 154 JP 440 so that it falls to the magistrates' court to fix any period of imprisonment or detention in default of payment of these amounts.

Fines imposed by coroners

A fine imposed by a coroner, or a recognisance forfeited at an inquest heard before a coroner, is to be treated for collection, enforcement and remission purposes as having been imposed by the magistrates' court acting for the area in which the coroner's court was held. After imposing the fine the coroner is required to give details of the fine to the magistrates' court clerk as soon as is practicable (CJA 1988, s 67). There is no prescribed form for giving such details to the clerk.

Financial penalty enforcement orders — Armed Forces

On entering the Armed Forces, a serviceman becomes subject to a code of Naval, Military or Air Force law, and various disciplinary provisions apply. While in the forces it is possible that a financial penalty may be awarded against a serviceman for an offence. Where this is so in relation to what is called a "qualifying offence", and the serviceman leaves the forces and is no longer subject to service law, the Defence Council (the authority responsible for exercising on behalf of the Crown the powers of command and administration over the Armed Forces) or a person authorised on behalf of the Defence Council may make a financial penalty enforcement order in respect of the outstanding sum. The order is then sent for registration to the magistrates' court acting for the area within whose jurisdiction the ex-serviceman appears to reside, or is likely to reside (Army Act 1955, s 133A(1); Air Force Act 1955, s 133A(1); Naval Discipline Act 1957, s 128F(1)).

The order when made will contain a certificate setting out details of the penalty and outstanding sum. Rule 47 of the Magistrates' Courts Rules 1981 requires the magistrates' court clerk receiving such an order to register it by means of a memorandum entered in the court register and then to send written notice to the Defence Council or authorised officer, stating that the order has been registered. Once the order is registered the clerk must serve notice of the registration on the ex-serviceman. The prescribed form of notice to the ex-serviceman is in Form 47 of the Magistrates' Courts (Forms) Rules 1981, and may be served by delivering it to him or sending it by post addressed to him at the address shown on the financial penalty enforcement order. Once the order is registered service enforcement procedures cease to be available for recovery of the outstanding sum and the penalty is enforced as if it were a fine imposed on conviction by the relevant magistrates' court.

Enforcement in the High Court and county court

Another option open to the magistrates' court clerk for the purpose of recovering outstanding sums is to take proceedings in the High Court or county court. The clerk may only do this after he has been duly authorised by a magistrates' court following an inquiry into the defendant's means (MCA 1980, s 87). The form of authority is contained in Form 63 of the Magistrates' Courts (Forms) Rules 1981.

The proceedings may be taken with regard to the amount outstanding as if in pursuance of a judgment or order of the High Court or county court. Proceedings will be taken in either the High Court or county court according to the size of the outstanding sum. If the sum exceeds the financial jurisdiction of the county court, proceedings should instead be brought in the High Court.

The remedies available in the High Court or county court are limited to proceedings for the attachment of debts owed to the defendant; garnishee proceedings; and the making of an order charging the defendant's land or the appointment of a receiver by way of equitable execution. A writ of *fieri facias* or other process against goods is excluded, as is imprisonment and attachment of earnings, since these are remedies available in the magistrates' court.

High Court procedure is governed by Rules of the Supreme Court Orders 49, 50 and 51, and in the county court by County Court Rules Orders 25, 27, 30 and 31.

It is for the justices' clerk to take the proceedings, which are made *ex parte* supported by affidavit. In the case of garnishee proceedings, the debtor's name must be set out together with the amount of the debt, if this is known. In special circumstances, a receiver may be appointed by way of equitable execution in lieu of garnishee proceedings, for example where the existence of debts is not known and there is no way of finding out *(Goldschmidt* v *Oberrheinische Metallwerke* [1906] 1 KB 373).

Fines on companies

Where a magistrates' court has adjudged a company by a conviction to pay a sum or is treated by any enactment as having done so, and the court has issued a warrant of distress for the purpose of levying the sum, and it appears on the return of the warrant that the company's money and goods are insufficient to satisfy the sum together with the costs and charges of levying the distress, the court clerk may apply for an administration order under section 9 of the Insolvency Act (IA) 1986. An administration order directs that while the order is in force, the company's business and property should be arranged by a person, called the administrator, appointed by the court for the purpose.

The clerk may also as an alternative petition for the winding-up of the company under section 124 of the IA 1986.

In either case there is no requirement that the clerk must first be authorised by a magistrates' court to take the proceedings. The clerk can then institute proceedings of his own motion.

Civilian enforcement officers

Courts are no longer required to enlist the support of police officers to execute warrants of arrest and warrants of commitment for non-payment of fines, etc. Section 125(2) of the MCA 1980 provides that a warrant of arrest, a warrant of commitment or warrant of distress issued for the recovery of an outstanding sum may be executed not only by a constable but also by a person who is:

(a) employed by a magistrates' courts Committee,
(b) authorised to execute such warrants,
(c) acting within the area for which the Courts' Committee that employs him performs its functions.

The form of authority is an authorisation in writing in a form suitable for identifying the civilian enforcement officer to persons with whom he deals as a person so authorised.

Authority is also given to execute warrants of committal to custody overnight at a police station for non-payment of a fine etc. (Magistrates' Courts (Civilian Fine Enforcement Officers) (No 2) Rules 1990).

CHAPTER 3

Non-Custodial Enforcement Measures

CHAPTER 3

Non-Custodial Enforcement Measures

Introduction

There are a variety of measures open to courts for recovering outstanding sums which fall short of imprisonment or detention in default of payment. It is imperative that each of these measures should be considered or tried prior to custody. The steps outlined below can be taken either at the time of conviction or at any time thereafter, subject to any requirement for the offender's attendance.

Money payment supervision orders

1. The Order

Where a person is required to pay a fine, costs, compensation or a forfeited recognisance, the court may, either at the time of conviction or at a later date, order him to be placed under the supervision of such person as the court appoints (MCA 1980, s 88). The making of the order is entirely at the court's discretion and may be made even where there is no default in payment. A money payments supervision order will be most appropriate in cases involving youths or where it appears that the support and encouragement of someone else at hand may be productive in recovering payment. Such an order may avoid the need to consider more severe remedies.

The order places upon the person appointed supervisor, the duty to advise and befriend the offender with a view to inducing him to pay the sum ordered and thereby avoid committal to prison for non-payment. The supervisor must provide the court with any information that may be required relating to the offender's conduct and means (Magistrates' Courts Rules 1981, r 56).

The supervisor in practice is generally a probation officer, but this need not always be so. The court has a discretion to appoint any person and may therefore appoint a close friend or relative, but the court should be satisfied with the suitability of the person it wishes to appoint before making such an appointment. Although a supervisor is under a duty to provide the court with information that may be requested, the court has no power to require the supervisor's appearance in court.

The consent of the offender to the making of an order is not required and, where an order is made on an occasion subsequent to the date of conviction, the offender's presence is not necessary. Should the court make an order in the offender's absence, the court clerk must deliver or send to the offender written notice of the appointment in the prescribed form (Magistrates' Courts Forms Rules 1981, Form 62). A copy of the notice should also be sent to the supervisor, although there is no requirement for this.

2. Cessation of order

Generally an order remains in force as long as the offender remains liable to pay any outstanding balance. The order ceases however on the making of a transfer of fine order. An order may also be discharged at any time by the court which made it, but this does not preclude the court from making a subsequent order (MCA 1980, s 88(3)).

3. Supervision and imprisonment or detention in default of payment

Where a supervision order is in force, the offender may not be committed to prison in default of payment of any outstanding sum unless the court has taken such steps as may be reasonably practicable to obtain from the supervisor an oral or written report of the offender's conduct and means (MCA 1980, s 88(6)). The report will provide the court with details of the defendant's behaviour, and of his income and expenditure throughout the period of supervision.

The fact that a person has been committed to prison in default of payment and the issue of the warrant of commitment postponed does not prevent the court making a money payments supervision order. However, in these circumstances the making of a money payments supervision order does not mean that a report must be obtained from the supervisor before the warrant of commitment can be issued in the event of default in the terms of the postponement, although it may be wise to do so. The requirement to obtain a report from the supervisor applies only at the stage when the term of imprisonment is originally fixed; it does not apply to the act of issuing the warrant in default of the terms of postponement (*R* v *Clerkenwell Stipendiary Magistrate, ex parte Mays* [1975] 1 All ER 65).

Young persons

With regard to persons aged under 21, a court may not commit such person to detention in default of paying an outstanding sum on a date subsequent to the date of conviction unless that person has been made the subject of a money payments supervision order, or the court is satisfied that it is undesirable or impracticable to place him under supervision (MCA 1980, s 88(4)).

Where the court does commit a person aged under 21 to detention in default of payment, without having placed him under supervision, the court must state in the warrant of commitment the grounds upon which it is satisfied that supervision is undesirable or impracticable (MCA 1980, s 88(5)).

Attendance centre orders

Where a court would have power to impose imprisonment for non-payment of an outstanding sum in the case of persons under 21 years of age, but for the statutory restrictions on imprisonment of such persons, the court may instead make an attendance centre order for a specified number of hours, provided that an attendance centre is available and reasonably accessible to the offender having regard to his age, the means of access available to him and any other circumstances (CJA 1982, s 17(1)).

An order can be made before a previous order has ceased to have effect (CJA 1982, s 17(6)). The court may determine the number of hours to be specified in the order without regard to the number of hours specified in the previous order, or to the fact that the order is still in force. An order may not be made in respect of a person under 18 years of age for default in payment for the balance outstanding unless the court has, since the conviction, inquired into his means in his presence on at least one occasion (MCA 1980, s 81(3A)).

Form 2 in the Magistrates' Courts (Attendance Centre) Rules 1992 is the prescribed form of order.

Number of hours

No guidance is given of the number of hours to be imposed relative to the amount of an outstanding sum, save that under section 17(4) and (5) of the CJA 1982:

(i) the aggregate number of hours should not be less than 12, except in relation to an offender under 14 , when the number of hours may be less than twelve if the court's opinion is that 12 hours would be excessive having regard to the child's age or any other circumstances;

(ii) the aggregate number of hours should not exceed 12 except where the court's opinion, having regard to all the circumstances, is that 12 hours would be inadequate, in which case the aggregate number of hours should not exceed 24 where the offender is aged under 16 years of age, or 36 hours where the offender is aged under 21, but not less than 16.

Notice of order

A copy of the order must be delivered or sent to the office in charge of the attendance centre. In addition a copy must be delivered to the offender or sent by registered or recorded delivery post to the offender's last or usual place of abode (CJA 1982, s 17(12)).

Payment received after order made

Where an attendance centre order has been made, payment of the whole sum outstanding will cause the order to cease to have affect (CJA 1982, s 17(13)). Payment of part only means that the total number of hours is reduced proportionately, i.e. by the number of complete hours which, in proportion to the amount paid, is approximate to (but does not exceed) the ratio of "hours : the sum" for which the order was first made (CJA 1982, s 17(13)(*b*)). For example, where 12 hours attendance was ordered for non-payment of £100, payment of £50 reduces the 12 hours to six.

Payment may be made as follows:

- payment of the whole sum to the court clerk which made the order, or
- payment of the whole, or part payment, to the officer in charge of the attendance centre specified in the order.

However, note that the officer in charge of the attendance centre need not accept a payment of part of the sum outstanding unless it is an amount required to secure a reduction of at least one complete hour or some multiple thereof.

Where the court clerk receives payment in full he must notify the officer in charge of the attendance centre (Magistrates' Courts (Attendance Centre) Rules 1992, r 3(3)).

Failure to comply with order

In the event of failure to comply with an attendance centre order, the court may revoke the order and deal with the defaulter in any way in which the court could have done so originally for the default in payment. It follows that a fresh order can be made although the merits of making such an order may be called into question given that a default has already been made. The alternative methods of enforcement of payment may be used instead including commitment in default of payment (except for persons aged under 18).

Remission

Once a fine has been imposed, then apart from any avenue of appeal it does not have to be the case that the total fine as originally imposed must be recovered whatever the circumstances. In appropriate cases it is open to the court to consider ordering that the fine be reduced in amount. Whether it is open to the court to remit amounts other than fines in the strict sense depends upon the proper construction of the relevant statutory provisions.

Section 150(1) of the MCA 1980 defines a "fine" as "... any pecuniary penalty or pecuniary forfeiture or pecuniary compensation payable under a conviction". The question arises whether this definition applies to forfeited recognisances and orders for compensation under section 35 of the PCCA 1973. As far as forfeited recognisances are concerned, the power to remit is specifically excluded by section 120(4) of the MCA 1980 with regard to compensation, orders made under section 35 of the PCCA 1983 are enforced as sums adjudged to be paid by conviction (Administration of Justice Act 1970 (AJA), s 41). The use of this expression would suggest that it is not intended that such orders are enforced in the same way as for fines, so that where reference is made in the MCA 1980 to "fines" as opposed to "sums adjudged to be paid by conviction" a different approach is intended. This being so it would appear that it is not possible to treat compensation ordered under section 35 of the PCCA 1973 as for a fine for remission purposes. Furthermore, separate provision exists to review orders for compensation (see below) which would otherwise be unnecessary if the power to remit was applicable.

Costs are clearly not within the definition of fines and so may not be remitted.

This being so, when dealing with fines in the strict sense, the court has power at any time to remit the whole or part of a fine as it thinks just to do so. However, the court may only exercise this power having regard to a change of circumstances which has occurred:

1. where the court is considering whether to issue a warrant of commitment after the issue of the warrant has been postponed, since the date when the date of the issue of the warrant was last postponed or the terms of postponement last varied, or
2. in any other case since the date of conviction.

It is a matter entirely for the court in the exercise of its judicial discretion whether to remit the whole or part of an outstanding sum. The exercise of the power can follow an application for the purpose made by the offender or his legal representative, or the court may proceed of its own motion (MCA 1980, s 85).

Where the court remits the whole or part of a fine after a term of imprisonment has been fixed, the court must also reduce proportionately the term of imprisonment (MCA 1980, s 85(2)).

However with regard to fines imposed by the Crown Court, the court's consent is required before a magistrates' court can remit the whole or part of a Crown Court fine which it is required to enforce.

Review of fines

Where a court fixes the amount of a fine where:

1. an offender is convicted in his absence or following a written notification of a plea of guilty and non-appearance, or
2. an offender or the parent or guardian of an offender who is a child or young person fails to comply with a financial circumstances order or has otherwise failed to co-operate with the court in its inquiry into his financial circumstances

then, on subsequently inquiring into the offender's financial circumstances, the court is satisfied that had it had the results of that inquiry when sentencing the offender it would

1. have fixed a smaller amount; or
2. not have fined him,

the court may remit the whole or any part of the fine. If this occurs after a term of imprisonment has been fixed, the court must reduce the term by the corresponding proportion. In calculating the reduction, any fraction of a day must be ignored.

The word "fine" would appear to be used in the narrow sense here, so that costs and compensation cannot be remitted under this provision.

Review of compensation

At any time before the whole amount of any compensation order has been paid, then, provided the period for any appeal has expired, a magistrates' court which has responsibility for enforcing the order (including a court of transfer) may discharge the order, or reduce the amount which remains to be paid, if it appears that

1. the injury, loss or damage has been held in civil proceeding to be less than it was taken to be for the purpose of the order; or
2. in the case of an order for the loss of property, that the property has been recovered by the person in whose favour the order was made; or
3. the means of the person against whom the order was made are insufficient to satisfy in full both the order and any confiscation order made under Part VI of the CJA 1988 made against him in the same proceedings; or
4. the person against whom the order was made has suffered a substantial reduction in his means which was unexpected at the time when the compensation order was made, and that his means seem unlikely to increase for a considerable period.

It would seem that 4. above would be the most likely circumstances in which an application was made to the court and could be combined with an application to remit fines also.

However where an order was made by the Crown Court, a magistrates' court must not exercise the powers 3. or 4. above unless the consent of the Crown Court has first been obtained.

An application for review of a compensation order must be made by way of complaint (Magistrates' Courts Rules 1981, r 104). The court clerk receiving the complaint must send a letter to the person entitled to the compensation inviting that person to make observations and to attend the hearing and to make representations.

Remission of recognisances

Although the power to remit fines does not extend to the remission of forfeited recognisances, a recognisance which has been forfeited can be remitted by a separate power contained in section 120(4) of the MCA 1980. By this provision, at any time before the issue of a warrant of commitment to enforce payment of the outstanding sum, or before the sale of goods under a warrant of distress to satisfy the outstanding sum, the court may remit the whole or any part of the sum outstanding either absolutely or under such conditions as the court thinks just. Again there would appear to be a complete discretion in the court to decide whether and in what circumstances the outstanding sum should be remitted.

Distress

Introduction

In recent years the use of distress warrants has undergone something of a resurgence, owing to a number of factors. First is perhaps an increasing reluctance by the police to become involved in the enforcement of debt of whatever description and latterly even to execute warrants of arrest. The second factor may be the creation of the fixed penalty system, which provides magistrates' courts with a large number of low value debts to enforce. Thirdly, the firms of private bailiffs themselves have not been slow to realise the commercial potential for growth and have marketed their services with increasing effectiveness. Finally, and perhaps most importantly, it should not be forgotten that the appeal courts have also encouraged a greater use of distress continuing to emphasise that custody is a last resort only after all other methods have failed (see for example *R* v *Birmingham Justices, ex parte Bennett* (1983) 147 JP 279). However, justices may properly require positive evidence that the defendant has goods before issuing a warrant of distress (*R* v *German* (1891) 5 JP 358).

The concept of distress is not new and it simply means the seizing of money and/or goods belonging to the debtor to satisfy his debt. The critics of the procedure claim that it is an anachronism more in keeping with the financial times of Dickens than that of the 1990s. The courts, however, whilst accepting that it is not an answer to all problems, see the use of distress as a significant weapon in the enforcement armoury. Unlike the county courts, magistrates' courts do not certify bailiffs so that firms of private bailiffs must be employed. While the police can execute warrants of distress by law, it is unlikely that they will be prepared to do so save in exceptional circumstances. One major benefit to the court of using private bailiffs is that they do not usually charge the court for their services, but simply add their costs of distress to the debt required to be collected. Unfortunately, not all distress warrants are successfully executed and many are returned "nulla bona", "no trace" or "sufficient goods potentially not achieved". There is currently much debate about whether courts should pay bailiffs costs in such cases as there is no provision as yet to meet these out of public funds. There is also debate over the control of the bailiffs' costs when added to the warrant of distress. The only control over bailiffs' costs is contained in section 78(5) of the MCA 1980, which provides that if a person charged with the execution of a distress warrant wilfully retains or otherwise extracts any other costs and charges than those properly payable, or makes any improper charge, he would be liable on summary conviction to a fine not exceeding £200. Whether a charge is properly payable or not is matter of fact determined by a magistrates' court. A fine of £200 may not be sufficient to deter bailiffs from charging improperly.

I. Issue and execution of distress warrants

The issue and execution of distress warrants is regulated by the Magistrates' Court Act 1980 (in particular s 76) and the Magistrates' Court Rules 1981. As in the case of imprisonment, the court has power to postpone the issue of a distress warrant until such time and on such conditions, if any, as the court thinks fit (MCA 1980, s 77(1)). Rule 54 of the Magistrates' Court Rules 1981 adds the necessary detail regarding the warrant's content and the method of execution, namely:

1. The warrant must name or otherwise describe the person against whom the distress is to be levied.
2. The warrant must be directed to the constable of the police area in which the warrant is issued or to the authorised persons for the police area specified in the warrant, or to a person named in the warrant, and shall require them to levy the sum in question by distress and sale of the goods belonging to the person in question.
3. The warrant may, where it is directed to the constables of a police area, instead of being executed by any of those constables, be executed by any person under the direction of a constable.
4. The warrant must authorise the person in charge with the execution of it to take, as well as goods, any money of the person against whom the distress is levied; and any money so taken shall be treated as if it were the proceeds of the sale of goods taken under the warrant.
5. The warrant must require the person charged with the execution to pay the sum levied to the clerk of the Court that issued the warrant. Any wilful retention of the proceeds (regardless of whatever offences were committed) is punishable by a fine (MCA 1980, s 78(5)).

6. Clothes or bedding of any person or his family or the tools and implements of his trade cannot be taken under the warrant. Note that water, gas and electricity fittings let for hire by the utility boards, and Crown property, cannot be the subject of distress.
7. The distress levied under the warrant must be sold within such period beginning not earlier than the sixth day after the making of the distress as may be specified in the warrant; or, if no period is specified in the warrant, within a period beginning on the sixth day and ending on the 14th day after the making of the distress. However, with the consent in writing of the person against whom the distress is levied, the distress may be sold sooner.
8. The distress must be sold by public auction or in such other manner as the person against whom the distress is levied may in writing allow.
9. The distress must not be sold if the sum for which the warrant was issued and the charges of taking and keeping the distress have been paid.
10. Subject to any direction to the contrary in the warrant, where the distress is levied on household goods, they cannot, without the consent in writing of the person against whom the distress is levied, be removed from the house until the day of sale. However the goods are impounded by affixing to them a conspicuous mark. Removing these goods, or defacing or removing the mark are offences (MCA 1980, s 78(4)).
11. The constable or bailiff charged with the warrant's execution must cause the distress to be sold, and may deduct out of the amount realised by the sale all costs and charges incurred in effecting the sale. He must then return to the owner a balance, after retaining the amount for which the warrant was issued and the proper costs and charges of the warrant's execution.
12. The constable or bailiff charged with the warrant's execution must, as soon as is practicable, send to the clerk of the court that issued it a written account of the costs and charges incurred in executing it. The clerk must allow the person against whom the distress was levied to inspect the account, at any reasonable time appointed by the court, within one month after the levy of the distress.
13. If any person pays or tenders to the constable or bailiff the sum mentioned in the warrant, or produces a receipt of that sum given by the clerk of the court that issued the warrant, and also pays the amount of the costs and charges of the distress up to the time of the payment or tender or the production of the receipt, the constable or bailiff must not execute the warrant, or must cease to execute it, as the case may be.

Despite the above requirements, if the warrant does contain any defect, this does not make it void provided the warrant states that the sum has been adjudged to be paid by the conviction or order of a magistrates' court (MCA 1980, s 78(1)). Similarly, a person acting under a warrant of distress is not deemed to be a trespasser by reason only of any irregularity in the warrant's execution.

In addition to the statutory requirements detailed above, many courts also have local policies, such as the taking of part payment by bailiffs, and imposing a time limit on the life of the warrant. These arrangements vary from area to area.

2. Special provisions for recovery of fines imposed on fishing boat master, crew etc

Where a fine is imposed by a magistrates' court in England and Wales or Northern Ireland on the master, owner, charterer or a crew member of a fishing boat who was convicted of an offence under section 5 or section 10 of the Sea Fisheries Act 1968, or section 2 of the Fishery Limits Act 1976, the court may:

(i) issue a warrant of distress against the boat, its gear, catch and any property of the person convicted, for the purpose of levying the amount of the fine; and

(ii) if the boat is a "foreign fishing boat" order it to be detained for a period not exceeding three months from the date of the conviction, or until the fine is paid, or the amount levied in pursuance of any distress warrant, whichever first occurs.

3. Scotland and the Isle of Man

A warrant of distress issued in England can be executed in Scotland if endorsed in accordance with the Summary Jurisdiction (Process) Act 1881. This also applies to the Isle of Man by virtue of the Summary Jurisdiction Process (Isle of Man) Order 1928.

4. Requirement to give notice of issue of distress warrant

The issue of a distress warrant is not subject to the restrictions which apply in the case of imprisonment. Inquiry into means is not a statutory requirement before the issue of a warrant of distress. It seems that all that is necessary to trigger the issue of the warrant is for there to be a failure to comply with the terms of the order for payment.

In the absence of any specific provision giving the offender the right to be heard prior to the issue of a warrant of distress, as compared with imprisonment, where there is an absolute requirement for a hearing before a warrant is issued on an occasion subsequent to conviction, it might be argued that there is then no such right before the issue of a distress warrant. However natural justice does seem to imply that there must be such a right. Lord Fraser, giving the leading judgment at the House of Lords in *Forrest* v *Brighton Justices* [1981] 2 All ER 711, said:

> *"One of the principles of natural justice is that a person is entitled to adequate notice and opportunity to be heard before any judicial order is pronounced against him, so that he, or someone acting on his behalf, may make such representations, if any, as he sees fit. This is the rule of audi alteram partem which applies to all judicial proceedings, unless its application to a particular class of proceedings has been excluded by Parliament expressly or by necessary implication."*

In *Bonaker* v *Evans* (1850) 16 QBD 162 it was said that:

> *"... no proposition can be more clearly established than that a man cannot incur the loss of liberty or property for an offence by a judicial proceeding until he has had a fair opportunity of answering the charge against him, unless the legislature has expressly or impliedly given an authority to act without that necessary preliminary."*

It is then a question of deciding whether the requirement to give notice has been excluded either expressly or by necessary implication. The requirement has certainly not been expressly excluded. Whether the requirement has been excluded by necessary implication is a matter of interpretation but with such an important and weighty matter under consideration i.e. the issue of a distress warrant, it would seem that the preferred argument should be that notice and a hearing is required. The problem can be easily overcome by the issue of a summons for the purpose of enforcement proceedings with a warning contained in the summons that the court could issue a warrant of distress. See also *R* v *Guildford Justices, ex parte Rich, The Times,* 17 May 1996 where it was held that notice had to be given before a distress warrant could be issued.

Form 48 in the Magistrates' Courts (Forms) Rules 1981 is the prescribed form of distress warrant. Form 49, where appropriate, is the prescribed form of return of insufficient distress.

5. Search of the person

Another useful power which can be exercised only when an offender is present in court is to search and to seize sums of money in the offender's possession. Where a magistrates' court has adjudged a person to pay a sum by conviction, the court may order him to be searched and any money found may, unless the court otherwise directs, be applied towards payment of the outstanding sum. Any balance must be returned to the individual. Furthermore any money found on the arrest of a person adjudged to pay a sum by a conviction, or on his being taken to a prison or other place of detention in default may be applied towards payment of the outstanding balance unless the court otherwise directs. Any direction so given must be noted on the warrant of commitment.

Money found in either of the above situations may not to be applied towards payment of the outstanding sum if the court is satisfied that the money does not belong to the offender or that its loss would be more injurious to his family than would his detention (MCA 1980, s 80).

6. Young persons

Although no form of custodial order may be made in respect of a person aged under 18 for default in payment of a sum outstanding, a court may instead, where it would have had power to commit to prison for default a person over 20 years of age, make any of the following orders:

1. An order requiring a parent or guardian to enter into a recognisance to ensure that the youth pays the amount due (MCA 1980, s 81(1)(a)). The parent or guardian must consent to the making of an order. If consent is not given, the parent or guardian in those circumstances cannot be committed to prison for withholding the consent as in the case of a failure to consent to entering into a recognisance to keep the peace and be of good behaviour. In the absence of consent it would appear that an order cannot be made.
2. An order directing that the amount outstanding be paid by the parent or guardian instead of by the youth (MCA 1980, s 81(1)(b)). Such an order may only be made if the court is satisfied in all the circumstances that it is reasonable to make the order. The amount outstanding is then enforced against the parent or guardian as if he had been convicted of the original offence (MCA 1980, s 81(7)). Furthermore an order under this provision may be made against a parent or guardian who, having been required to attend, has failed to do so; however where a parent does attend an order should not be made without giving

the parent or guardian an opportunity of being heard (MCA 1980, s 81(5)).

Neither of the above orders can be made unless the court is satisfied that the youth who has defaulted has had since the date on which the sum in question was ordered, the means to pay the outstanding sum or any instalment of it, and he has refused or neglected to pay it.

In the case of an order made under **2.** above, a parent or guardian may appeal to the Crown Court against the making of the order.

A guardian in the context of the above means a person appointed according to law to be a guardian, or by an order of the court of competent jurisdiction.

An order can be made in respect of fines, costs, compensation or a forfeited recognisance. Note that section 55 of the Children and Young Persons Act 1933, as amended, provides that where a child or young person is convicted or found guilty of an offence and is ordered to pay a fine, costs or compensation, it is the court's duty to order that the amount imposed should be paid by the parent or guardian instead of by the child unless the court is satisfied that:

1. that the parent or guardian cannot be found; or
2. that it would be unreasonable to make an order for payment, having regard to the circumstances of the case.

A child is a person aged under 14, young person means a person who has attained the age of 14 years and is under the age of 18 years.

With regard to a young person who has attained the age of 16 years, the duty to order that a parent or guardian, rather than the young person, should pay any sum imposed, is replaced by a power only to make such an order.

CHAPTER 4

Imprisonment and Detention for Non-Payment of Fines

CHAPTER 4

Imprisonment and Detention for Non-payment of Fines

Introduction

"Offenders generally and young offenders in particular ought not to be locked up for non-payment of fines unless no sensible alternative presents itself." (*In re Cawley & Others* (1996) 160 JP 133.)

Although a magistrates' court has power ultimately to order imprisonment for default in paying an outstanding sum, subject to certain pre-conditions (MCA 1980, s 76), it is a step which should not be taken lightly. There are other methods of enforcement which can and must be considered first. Indeed in *R* v *Birmingham Justices, ex parte Bennett* (1983) 147 JP 279 it was said that should there be a reasonable likelihood that a defendant has assets available to satisfy the sum he owes, magistrates should proceed by way of a distress warrant rather than by committing him to prison. Although this case concerned only costs and compensation, it is submitted that the approach is equally valid for fines.

Once the stage has been reached where there is no alternative but to impose imprisonment, the court should seek to impose the shortest possible term which can adequately deal with the situation. The maximum periods of imprisonment which may be imposed for non-payment of a sum outstanding are contained in Schedule 4 of the MCA 1980 (see below) and vary according to the amount outstanding. It is of the greatest importance to recognise that the terms of imprisonment are expressed as maxima. Courts should adopt a flexible approach and impose shorter periods where circumstances permit. Among the matters which the court could take into account may be that the defaulter has never been in prison before; or that the fine was imposed for an offence which does not itself carry imprisonment as a penalty; or that the amount outstanding is towards the lower end of the band for the respective period of imprisonment.

The maximum periods of imprisonment which may be imposed under Schedule 4 in the event of non-payment are as follows:

An amount not exceeding £200	7 days
An amount exceeding £200 but not exceeding £500	14 days
An amount exceeding £500 but not exceeding £1,000	28 days
An amount exceeding £1,000 but not exceeding £2,500	45 days
An amount exceeding £2,500 but not exceeding £5,000	3 months
An amount exceeding £5,000 but not exceeding £10,000	6 months
An amount exceeding £10,000	12 months

Where the amount due at the time imprisonment is imposed has not been reduced by a part payment, then the respective periods of imprisonment set out above apply. However where there is a part payment before imprisonment is imposed, then separate provisions apply (see below).

Consecutive periods of imprisonment

Consecutive periods of imprisonment may be imposed subject to a maximum period of six months. Where however two or more periods of imprisonment are imposed for non-payment of fines, in respect of offences triable either way, the aggregate of the terms so imposed may exceed six months, but must not exceed 12 months. The limitation does not operate to reduce the aggregate of the terms which may be imposed below that which could be imposed in respect of any one of the outstanding sums (MCA 1980, s 133).

Should the court wish to impose consecutive terms of imprisonment for a number of outstanding fines, and the aggregate period of imprisonment to be imposed exceeds that which could have been imposed had the total of the individual fines been imposed as a single amount, then separate warrants of commitment must be issued. To impose consecutive periods of imprisonment, it is not sufficient to use a single warrant setting out details of different periods of imprisonment. All that this will achieve is for the aggregate period of imprisonment to be reduced to that applicable to the totalled sum of the outstanding fines. This is the effect of two High Court decisions: *R* v *Southampton Justices, ex parte Davis* [1981] 1 All ER 722 and *R* v *Midhurst Justices, ex parte Seymour* (1983) 147 JP 266.

In *Seymour* the court outlined the approach to be followed by justices; it was said that they must look at the whole of the circumstances, including the offences for which the fines were imposed and the amounts sought to be enforced. If satisfied that justice could be done by imposing a term not exceeding the statutory maximum, it is appropriate to do so on a single sheet. If, after full consideration, it is felt right that the aggregate of sentences imposed should exceed the maximum, separate warrants should be issued for each committal.

Postponement of issue of warrant

On imposing imprisonment or detention for an outstanding sum, the court may, if it thinks it expedient to do so, fix the term of imprisonment or detention and then postpone the issue of the warrant of commitment until such time and upon such conditions, if any, as the court thinks just (MCA 1980, s 77(2)). Whether it is expedient to postpone the issue of the warrant is a matter within the court's discretion.

Where the court exercises the power to postpone the issue of the warrant on terms, then on subsequent default it is necessary to hold a hearing to consider the issue of the warrant.

Generally the offender must be present before the court may issue the commitment warrant (MCA 1980, s 82(5)).

A summons or warrant may be issued to secure the offender's appearance (see below) (MCA 1980, s 83(1)).

However where the offender does not appear, the court may issue the warrant in absence provided the clerk has first served on the offender a notice in writing stating that the court intends to hold a hearing to consider whether to issue the commitment warrant and giving reasons why the court so intends (MCA 1980, s 82(5A)). The time for the hearing must not be earlier than 21 days after the issue of the notice, except that the court may at the time of imposing imprisonment and postponing the issue of the warrant, issue a notice in which case the hearing to consider the issue of the warrant may be at any time on any day following the end of the period for which the issue of the warrant of commitment had been postponed. In the event of non-appearance the warrant can then be issued without more (MCA 1980, s 82(5D)). Form 53B in the Magistrates' Courts (Forms) Rules 1981 is the prescribed form of notice.

The notice must state the time and place appointed for the hearing and also inform the offender that if he considers that there are grounds why the warrant should not be issued he may make representations to the court in person or in writing. However the court may exercise its powers in relation to the issue of a warrant whether or not the offender makes such representations (MCA 1980, s 82(5C))

The service of the notice is deemed to be served on the person if it is sent by registered post or recorded delivery service, addressed to him at his last known address, notwithstanding that the notice may be returned as undelivered or is for any other reason not received by that person (MCA 1980, s 82(5F)).

Where the court proceeds to hold a hearing to consider whether to issue the warrant, it is required under section 82(5B) of the MCA 1980 to consider such information about the offender's means as is available unless it has previously

1. inquired into the offender's means, and
2. postponed the issue of the warrant.

Variation of terms of postponed commitment

It had been accepted for some time that once a magistrates' court had exercised its powers under section 77(2) of the MCA 1980, to fix a term of imprisonment or detention and then to postpone the issue of the warrant of commitment, thereafter no power existed to review the terms of the postponement in the event of further default of a change in circumstances. In *R* v *Colchester Justices, ex parte Wilson* [1985] 2 All ER 97 it was held by the House of Lords that this was no longer the case. It was said that a magistrates' court could indeed exercise the power contained in section 77(2) as often as the justices considered appropriate. Lord Roskill said that:

> *"... there was no reason why the powers given by Section 77(2) should not be exercised from time to time and indeed as often as the justices concerned considered that the occasion required. So to hold was not to encourage or facilitate deliberate and inexcusable default; no doubt courts would be alert to see that the existence of the power further to postpone was not abused but was only exercised as the occasion required."*

Of earlier cases in which it had been held that the power did not exist, it was said that they had been wrongly decided. The decision, however, goes further than merely stating that a magistrates' court could indeed vary the terms of a postponed commitment. Their Lordships referred to the requirements of natural justice and to the comments of Lord Fraser in

Forrest v *Brighton Justices* (see p 33 above). Although the power to vary the terms of a postponed commitment is now in statutory form following an amendment to section 77, it is appropriate to say that the statutory provision, explained below, applies only to the issue of a commitment warrant. Where a distress warrant is ordered and the issue postponed on terms, it would seem that on the basis of *R* v *Colchester Justices,* there is power to vary the terms of postponement and as often as the court would wish. Section 77 of the MCA 1980 as amended, allows a magistrates' court to vary the terms of a postponed commitment. The court may:

1. direct that the issue of the commitment warrant shall be postponed until a time different from that to which it was previously postponed; or
2. vary any of the conditions on which it was postponed.

The court may only exercise these powers if it thinks just to do so having regard to a change of circumstances which has occurred since

a. where neither of the powers have been exercised previously, the date when the issue of warrant was postponed, and
b. in any other case, the date of the exercise or latest exercise of either or both of the above powers **1.** or **2.**

The exercise of either power may be as a result of the court acting of its own motion or following an application by the defaulter. Where the issue of a warrant has been postponed and it appears to a justice of the peace acting for the area in which the warrant has been or would have been issued that, since the date when the warrant was postponed or since the latest date of the exercise of the power to vary the terms of postponement, there has been a change of circumstances which would make it just for the court to exercise its powers to vary the terms of postponement, the justice must refer the application to the court (MCA 1980, s 77(5)).

Where such an application is referred to the court, it is the court clerk's duty to fix a time and place for the application to be heard and to give to the applicant notice of the time and place which he fixes (MCA 1980, s 77(6)). Form 53A in the Magistrates' Courts (Forms) Rules 1981 is the prescribed form of notice.

Where notice has been given but the applicant does not appear, the court may consider the application in his absence.

Where however a commitment warrant has been issued before the hearing of the application, the court has power to order that the warrant will cease to have effect and, if the applicant has been arrested in pursuance of the warrant, to order that he should be released. However the court must only make an order that the warrant shall cease if it is satisfied that the change of circumstances on which the applicant relies was not put before the court when it was determining whether to issue the warrant (MCA 1980, s 77(8)).

Imprisonment at time of conviction

As seen on page 6, the court may order imprisonment at the same time as it convicts the offender and imposes a fine or other payment. However the court under section 82 of the MCA 1980 may only impose imprisonment at the time of conviction in the following circumstances:

1. in the case of an offence punishable with imprisonment, where the offender appears to the court to have sufficient means to pay the sum forthwith;
2. where it appears to the court that the offender is unlikely to remain long enough at a place of abode in the United Kingdom to enable payment of the sum to be enforced by other methods;
3. where on the occasion of the conviction the court sentences the offender to immediate imprisonment, detention in a young offender institution for that or another offence; or
4. the offender is already serving a sentence of custody or detention in a young offender institution or detention in default of payment.

Note that the court is also precluded at the time of conviction from fixing a term of imprisonment to be served in the event of future default and postponing the issue of the warrant unless it has power to impose imprisonment forthwith as above (MCA 1980, s 82(2)).

Form 51 in the Magistrates' Courts (Forms) Rules 1981 is the prescribed form of warrant of commitment. Where the court commits under **1.** to **4.** above, this must be stated and the ground specified and entered in the warrant (MCA 1980, s 82(6)).

Imprisonment on occasion after date of conviction

Where imprisonment in default of payment is not imposed at the time of conviction, it may be imposed at a later date, but only if:

1. the offender is already serving a term of imprisonment or detention; or

2. the court has, since the conviction, inquired into the offender's means in his presence on at least one occasion.

(MCA 1980, s 82(3)). Form 52 in the Magistrates' Courts (Forms) Rules 1981 is the prescribed form of warrant of commitment.

1. Offender serving term of imprisonment or detention

Where the offender is already serving a term of imprisonment or detention, the court has power to commit to prison in default. However, the court may not commit in the offender's absence unless a notice of the hearing has been served on him. The notice must state the time and place of the hearing and inform the offender that he may make representations to the court in person or in writing why the warrant should not be issued. The notice and the requirements of the notice are the same as for a notice required on default in the terms of a postponed commitment (see p 41) (MCA 1980, s 82(5A)).

Should the court decide to commit the offender to prison, any period of imprisonment (not detention) may be either consecutive or concurrent to the term being served. Detention may be concurrent only.

2. Means inquiry required

Where the offender is not serving a term of imprisonment or detention as in **1.** above, and he has defaulted in this payment, then before imprisonment or detention can be imposed an inquiry into means is necessary.

Where the court inquires into an offender's means, it may not, on that occasion or at any time thereafter impose imprisonment for default in payment unless:

1. the offence to which the sum relates is punishable with imprisonment, and the defaulter appears to the court to have sufficient means to pay the sum forthwith; or
2. the court is satisfied that the default is due to the offender's wilful refusal or culpable neglect, and the court has considered or tried all other methods of enforcing payment and it appears to the court that they are inappropriate or unsuccessful (MCA 1980, s 82(4)).

The methods of enforcing payment which have to be considered are as follows:

- a distress warrant
- an application to the High Court or county court for enforcement

- a money payments supervision order
- an attachment of earnings order
- where the offender is aged under 21, an attendance centre order (MCA 1980, s 82(4A)).

Where the court imposes imprisonment without considering any of these methods, it would appear that the High Court will quash the warrant of commitment. (See for example, *R* v *Exeter City Justices, ex parte Sugar* (1992) 157 JP 766, where the High Court quashed a commitment, the magistrates' court not having considered the making of a money payments supervision order. See also *In re Cawley and Others* (1996) 160 JP 133 where it was said that each option must be considered and reasons given for its rejection.) The reasons for rejection must be stated in open court and ought properly to be entered in the court register as well as the warrant of commitment.

Although the above list appears to be exhaustive, an order for deduction from income support is not included which is an alternative method of recovering payments. It may be argued that the list is not exhaustive and that before committing a defaulter for non-payment, courts should consider whether deduction from income support is appropriate in addition to the methods set out above. Support for this argument may be gained from *R* v *Norwich Magistrates' Court, ex parte Tigger (formerly Lilly)* (1987) 151 JP 689. Here a magistrates' court had inquired into an offender's means and satisfied itself that the default in payment was due to wilful refusal or culpable neglect, but had not on the evidence discharged its duty to consider or try all other methods of enforcement before issuing a commitment warrant. The committal warrants were therefore quashed. It was also held that, when considering a defendant's means, it was incumbent upon the justices to ascertain whether the prosecution still held any assets belonging to the offender. In *R* v *Clacton Justices and Another, ex parte Commissioners of Customs and Excise* (1987) 152 JP 129, a fine of £10,000 was owing, but unbeknown to the justices, some £20,000 was still in the possession of the prosecution. The Court of Appeal held that it was quite plain, on the authority of *R* v *Birmingham Justices, ex parte Bennett* (1983), that the justices had failed properly to exercise their discretion when issuing the warrant of commitment, in not considering the defendant's means and ascertaining whether the prosecution held any of his assets.

Form 52 in the Magistrates' Court (Forms) Rules 1981 is the prescribed form of commitment warrant. The court must state the grounds for its decision and cause these to be entered in the court register as well as the warrant of commitment (MCA 1980, s 82(6)).

Offender's attendance at means inquiry

A court may not issue a commitment warrant except where the offender is present unless:

1. the court has previously fixed a term of imprisonment and postponed the issue of the warrant; or
2. the offender is serving a sentence of custody or detention in a young offender institution or detention in default.

Power to secure attendance at means inquiry or hearing to consider issue of commitment warrant

For the purpose of securing an offender's attendance at a means inquiry or at a hearing at which the court is to consider the issue of a commitment warrant the court may under section 83 of the MCA 1980:

1. issue a summons requiring his attendance; or
2. issue a warrant for his arrest

Where a summons has been issued if the offender fails to appear the court may issue a warrant for his arrest. Any warrant so issued ceases to have effect when the outstanding sum is paid to the police officer holding the warrant (or civilian enforcement officer).

Form 53 in the Magistrates' Courts (Forms) Rules 1981 is the prescribed form of summons. Form 54 is the prescribed form of warrant for arrest.

Power of court to fix date for appearance of offender at means inquiry

Where the court has exercised its power to dispense with immediate payment, it may on the occasion of exercising that power, or later, fix a day upon which the offender must appear in person before the court for the purposes of:

1. an inquiry into means to determine whether to impose imprisonment; or
2. a hearing to determine whether to issue a warrant of commitment.

The offender's appearance is conditional on his failure to pay any instalment which has been ordered and has become due or any failure to pay within the time allowed. The court may only exercise this power in the offender's presence except that where a date has already been fixed, the court may fix a later day in substitution for the date previously fixed, and may do so in the offender's absence.

On a failure of a person to appear in person before the court, the court may issue a warrant of arrest (MCA 1980, s 86 (4)).

Power to require statement of means

Where a magistrates' court proposes to hold a means inquiry then either before or on enquiring into a person's means, the court may order the defaulter to furnish to the court within a specified period, such a statement of means as the court may require. It is at the court's discretion to decide what particulars of means are to be provided.

Before the means inquiry takes place, a Justice of the Peace or justices' clerk also has power to order that an offender furnish to the court within a specified period a statement of means (MCA 1980, s 84).

A person who fails to comply with an order to provide a statement of means is liable on summary conviction to a fine not exceeding £1,000.

If a person in furnishing a statement of means, makes a statement which he knows to be, or recklessly furnishes a statement which is false in a material particular, or knowingly fails to disclose any material fact, he is liable on summary conviction to imprisonment for a term not exceeding four months or a fine not exceeding £1,000 or both.

Effect on period of imprisonment of part-payment

Where imprisonment has been imposed, any payment will have an effect on the period to be served. If payment in full of the outstanding sum is made, this will cause the order to cease to have effect and, if the person is in custody, he must be released unless he is in custody for some other reason (MCA 1980, s 79(1)). Payment of part-only of the outstanding sum will reduce, but not erase, the period of imprisonment which is to be served. Part payment after imprisonment imposed will therefore have the effect of reducing any period of custody. However, it may be that before imprisonment has been imposed a part-payment has been made, in this case the period of imprisonment to be imposed at the outset is reduced.

1. Part-payment before imprisonment imposed

Where a part-payment of a sum outstanding is made before imprisonment is imposed, the maximum period of imprisonment which may be imposed in relation to the balance outstanding is that which is applicable to the original sum (see table, page 39) reduced by such number of days as bears to the total number of days the same proportion as the part-payment bears to the whole sum (MCA 1980, Paragraph 2(1) Schedule 4).

Any fraction of a day is left out of account in making this calculation, and the period cannot be reduced to less than five days whatever the amount of the part payment even though the period remaining to be served may be calculated to less than five days (Paragraph 2(2) Schedule 4 MCA 1980).

As an example X is originally fined £125 plus £25 costs, making a total of £150. The court may aggregate these sums for the purpose of imposing one period of imprisonment so that X could be imprisoned for non-payment of a total of £150 which would be for seven days. However X pays £50 before the means inquiry, leaving a balance of £100 to be paid, (i.e. two-thirds of the total). Seven days must therefore be reduced in proportion to the amount paid (i.e. one-third of the total), it is then necessary to deduct one-third of seven days (i.e. two and one-third days), but in calculating the reduction a fraction of a day is omitted. Therefore seven days is reduced by two days remaining to be served.

2. Part-payment after imprisonment has been imposed

Where part-payment has been made after imprisonment has been imposed, the period of imprisonment is reduced, but on this occasion by such number of days as bears to the total number of days imposed, less one day, the same proportion as the part-payment bears to the amount outstanding at the time imprisonment was imposed. In making the necessary reduction, any fraction of a day must not be taken into account (MCA 1980, s 79(2)).

By way of example, X is originally fined £300. He pays £50 and then defaults in payment. He is committed to prison in default of payment of £250. The period of imprisonment of 14 days is reduced proportionately by the part payment as above to 12 days (i.e. one-sixth payment reduces the payment by one-sixth, leaving fractions of a day out of the count).

The issue of the commitment warrant is then postponed on payment of £20 per week. X only pays a further £50 and the warrant falls to be issued.

In this case the period of imprisonment is then calculated as follows:

$$\frac{50 \times 11 \text{ days } (12 - 1)}{250} = 2 \text{ days}$$

Again fractions of days are omitted and the commitment warrant will be issued for ten days, (i.e. twelve minus two).

3. Minimum period of imprisonment

Where a part-payment has been made before imprisonment has been imposed under **1.** above, any reduction will not reduce the maximum period to less than seven days (MCA 1980, Sched 4, para 2(2)).

The minimum period of imprisonment which may be imposed is five days (MCA 1980, s 132). However in calculating a reduction under **2.** above, the commitment warrant may be issued for less than five days, the court at that stage is not imposing imprisonment but taking the step of issuing the warrant.

Receipt of payment after imprisonment has been imposed

Once imprisonment has been imposed, the persons authorised to receive payments made to discharge the debt under rule 55 of the Magistrates' Courts Rules 1981 are as follows:

1. Unless a commitment warrant has already been issued, the clerk of the enforcing court or the supervisor appointed under any fine supervision order.
2. Where the issue of a commitment warrant has been suspended on conditions which provide for payment to be made to the clerk of some other magistrates' court, that clerk.
3. Any constable holding the commitment warrant or where the warrant is directed to some other person (civilian enforcement officer), that person.
4. The governor or keeper of the prison or place in which the defaulter is detained, or other person having lawful custody of the defaulter.

Detention for short periods

1. Detention for one day in the courthouse or police station

Where the court has power, or would have power, to impose imprisonment or detention in default of payment but for the statutory restrictions relating to imprisonment or detention, the court may instead order a person to be detained within the precincts of the courthouse or at any police station until such hour, not later than eight o'clock in the evening of the day in which the order is made, as the court may direct. If the court makes such an order, it must not commit to prison or order detention in default (MCA 1980, s 135).

It is not necessary to allow time for payment or to hold a means inquiry before an order is made. Nor need any of the other restrictions relating to imprisonment or detention in default of payment be complied with. The provision cannot be used in the case of persons aged under 18.

2. Detention overnight in police station

Here, as above, the court may, instead of imposing imprisonment or detention in default of payment, issue a warrant for the offender's detention in a police station (MCA 1980, s 136). The restrictions which relate to the imposition of imprisonment or detention in default of payment do not apply.

A warrant issued for such detention authorises any police constable or any other person (civilian enforcement officer) who is:

1. employed by a Magistrates' Court Committee;
2. authorised in the prescribed manner to execute such warrants; and
3. acting within the area for which the authority that employs him performs its functions

to arrest the defaulter and to take him to a police station. The warrant requires the officer in charge of the station to detain the defaulter until eight o'clock on the morning of the day following that on which he is arrested, or if he is arrested between midnight and eight o'clock in the morning, until eight o'clock in the morning of the day on which he is arrested. The officer in charge of the station may, however, release the offender at any time within four hours before eight o'clock in the morning if he thinks it expedient to do so to enable the offender to go to work, or for any other reason appearing to the officer to be sufficient (MCA 1980, s 136). Form 58 in the Magistrates' Courts (Forms) Rules 1981 is the prescribed form of warrant.

The power cannot be used in relation to persons aged under 18.

Execution in different parts of the United Kingdom of warrants for imprisonment for non-payment

1. Scotland

A warrant issued in England and Wales committing a person to prison for non-payment of fine, may be executed in Scotland by any constable appointed for a police area, as if the warrant were an extract conviction for imprisonment issued in Scotland in default of payment of the fine (Criminal Law Act 1977, s 38A). A person arrested by virtue of this provision can be detained in any prison in Scotland, and while he is so detained he is to be treated for all purposes as if he were detained under an extract conviction issued in Scotland. Execution of the warrant may take place whether or not it has been endorsed under section 4 of the Summary Jurisdiction (Process) Act 1881.

2. Northern Ireland

A warrant issued in England and Wales committing a person to prison for non-payment of a fine may be executed in Northern Ireland by a member of the Royal Ulster Constabulary as if it were a warrant committing him to prison in default of payment of the sum adjudged to be paid by a conviction in Northern Ireland (Criminal Law Act 1977, s 38B). A person arrested by virtue of this provision may be detained in any prison in Northern Ireland and while he is so detained he is to be treated for all purposes as if he were detained under a warrant of commitment issued in Northern Ireland.

3. England and Wales

Similar provisions exist for the execution in England and Wales of warrants of commitment for non-payment of fines issued in Scotland and Northern Ireland.

Young persons

"To send a young person into custody, sometimes following an offence not itself punishable by custody, with all that that involves, not only for the defaulter but in the way of prison overcrowding and public expense (cancellation of the fine apart), is no small thing." (*In re Cawley and Others* (1996) 160 JP 133 at p 152.)

1. Introduction

There is no form of custodial sentence available for non-payment of fines and other sums in respect of persons aged under 18. For those between 18 and 21 years of age, detention in default of payment is available, although imprisonment is not (CJA 1982, ss 1 and 9).

The options available for an under 18 are therefore very limited. This should then operate to concentrate the minds of justices when imposing financial penalties on this age group. Whenever possible the most appropriate course should be to order a parent or guardian to pay a fine instead of the child or young person so that in the event of default enforcement proceedings are brought against an adult.

One of the questions often posed when enforcement proceedings are considered against the under 18s is whether the hearing should take place in a youth court or magistrates' mourt? Where the defaulter is aged under 18 and has responsibility for paying the outstanding sum, enforcement proceedings should be taken in a youth court and a summons issued to any parent or guardian. Where an adult is made responsible for payment of the young person's financial penalty, proceedings should be brought in a magistrates' court.

2. Detention in default of payment

Although no term of imprisonment may be imposed on a person aged under 21, where but for this restriction a court would have had power to commit such person to prison for non-payment, it may instead, where he is not less than 18 years of age, commit him to be detained in default of payment or may make an order fixing a term of detention in the event of future default, for a term not exceeding the term of imprisonment (CJA 1982, s 9). Before the court can exercise either of these powers:

1. The conditions required to be satisfied before imprisonment can be imposed for default in payment generally must be satisfied (see p 43);
2. The offender must have been placed under supervision unless the court is satisfied that it is undesirable or impracticable and where so satisfied must state the grounds on which it is so satisfied in the commitment warrant. (MCA 1980, s 88(4)(5) see also *In re Cawley and Others* (1996) 160 JP 133.)
3. The court must be of the opinion that no other method of dealing with the offender is appropriate. In forming this opinion, the court must take into account all such information about the circumstances of the default (including aggravating or mitigating factors) as is available, and may take into account

any information about the person which is before it (CJA 1982, s 1(5));

4. Where the court does commit to detention for default in payment, it must state in open court the reason for its opinion that no other method of dealing with the offender is appropriate. Any reason stated in accordance with this requirement must be specified in the commitment warrant and entered in the court's register (CJA 1982, s 1(5A)).

The court must consider all options to detention contained in section 82(4A) of the MCA 1980 (see above p xx) and provide reasons for the rejection of each. (See *In re Cawley and Others* at p 152).

An order that a person be detained in default of payment is an order that such person be detained in:

- a remand centre,
- a young offender institution, or
- any place in which a person 21 years or over could be imprisoned or detained for default in payment or a fine or any other sum of money,

as the Secretary of State may from time to time direct.

Form 52 in the Magistrates' Courts (Forms) Rules 1981 is the prescribed warrant of commitment.

3. Reduction for part-payment

Any payment in respect of the outstanding sum will reduce any period of detention in the same way as in the case of imprisonment.

4. Consecutive periods of detention

There appears to be no direct statutory authority to the effect that consecutive periods of detention for default in payment can be imposed. To conclude that there is power to impose consecutive periods of detention in default, it is necessary to find some legal basis for such a proposition.

Consideration may first be given to the general power to impose imprisonment in default contained in section 6 of the MCA 1980 which is extended by section 133 of the MCA 1980 to include power to impose consecutive periods of imprisonment for default in payment of fines etc. Section 1 of the CJA 1982 prohibits imprisonment entirely for the under 21s. Power to impose imprisonment for default and thereby the power to impose consecutive periods of imprisonment are expressly excluded because imprisonment is not available for the under 21s at all. However, section 9 of the CJA 1982 goes on to provide that where but for the general restriction on imposing imprisonment in the case of under 21s, there would have been power to commit a person under 21 but not less than 18 years of age to prison, then instead, a court has power to commit an individual to be detained for a "term" not exceeding the term of imprisonment.

The decision whether consecutive periods of detention in default can be imposed rests then upon the interpretation of the word "term" as used in section 9 of the CJA 1982. If it can be interpreted to include consecutive periods of imprisonment then consecutive periods of detention in default may be ordered. However a better view appears to be that the word "term" does not include consecutive periods of imprisonment because all that section 133 of the MCA 1980 does is to provide that terms of imprisonment may be imposed consecutively to one another. The expression "term of imprisonment" therefore, as set out in section 9 of the CJA 1982, will not apply to consecutive periods of imprisonment and in such case, as there is no other statutory provision enabling consecutive periods of detention in default to be imposed, there is no power to order that periods of detention in default of payment can be imposed consecutively.

The flowchart on page 56 may be helpful. From this you will see the different steps needed before a court can commit in default. There are basically three routes:

1. Where the defaulter is already in custody or detention;
2. Where the court has previously fixed a term of imprisonment and postponed the issue of the warrant;
3. Where a means inquiry must be held.

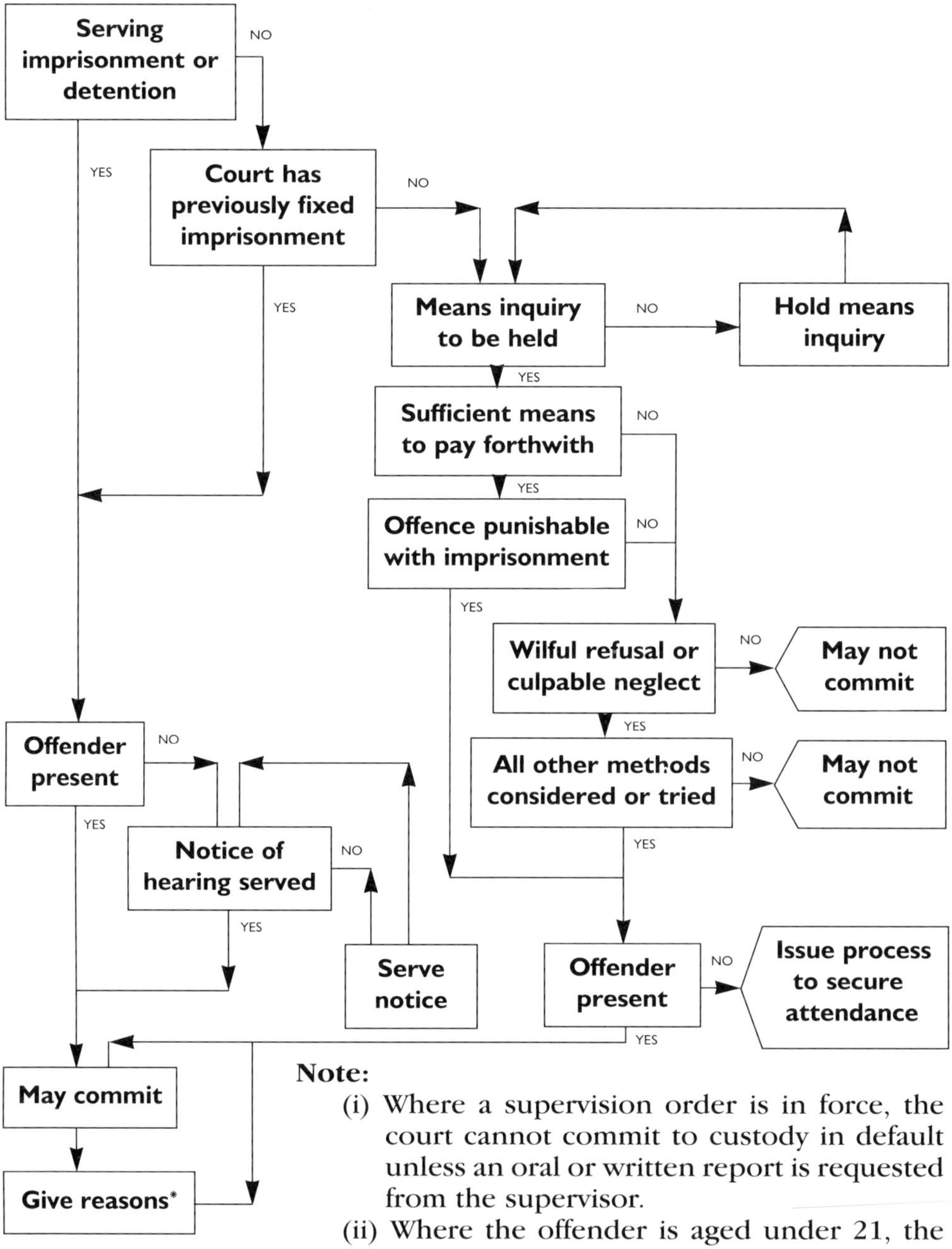

Note:

(i) Where a supervision order is in force, the court cannot commit to custody in default unless an oral or written report is requested from the supervisor.

(ii) Where the offender is aged under 21, the court cannot commit to detention in default unless a supervision order has been made or the court has good reasons for not doing.

*see also Appendix 1

PART 2: ENFORCEMENT OF CONFISCATION ORDERS

CHAPTER 5

Confiscation Orders

CHAPTER 5

Confiscation Orders

Drug trafficking

1. Power to make an order

Section 2 of the Drug Trafficking Act 1994 (DTA) requires the Crown Court, on convicting an offender of a drug trafficking offence (defined in Section 1(3) of the 1994 Act), to make a confiscation order where a defendant has benefited from drug trafficking. A person is taken to have benefited from drug trafficking if he has at any time received any payment or other reward in connection with drug trafficking, carried on by him or another person. The Crown Court must then make an order that there shall be recovered from the defendant an amount which it assesses to be the value of the defendant's proceeds of drug trafficking.

The amount to be recovered from a defendant under a confiscation order is assessed in accordance with Section 4 of the 1994 Act. The amount ordered is then enforced by a magistrates' court in the same way as a Crown Court fine. A period of imprisonment in default of payment must be ordered by the Crown Court by reference to the table contained in section 31(3A) of the PCCA 1973. Any commitment warrant issued for non-payment of the amount ordered under a confiscation order must run consecutively with any period of imprisonment, youth custody or detention which the defendant is liable to serve for the original drug trafficking offence or offences, including imprisonment or detention in default of payment of a fine imposed by the Crown Court for the original offence or offences, except where the warrant of commitment for non-payment has not been issued in which case this period is to be disregarded (DTA 1994, s 9).

Where an order has been made in respect of a person aged under 18 years of age, a magistrates' court cannot make an order that a parent or guardian should enter a recognisance to ensure payment or directing that the parent or guardian should pay the balance of the outstanding sum (DTA 1994, s 9(4)(a)). Furthermore an amount ordered to be paid by way of a confiscation order may not be remitted by a magistrates' court as in the case of fines generally (DTA 1994, s 9(4)(b)). However, the party liable to make payment can instead apply to the Crown Court for the amount ordered to be reduced, but this can only be done following an application to the High Court made by the defendant (or receiver) for a certificate that the realisable property is inadequate for the payment of any amount to be recovered under the confiscation order. Where a certificate has been issued then application can be made to the Crown Court (see generally DTA 1994, s 17).

Interest is also payable on sums which are not paid when ordered to be paid. The amount of interest is that for the time being applying to a civil judgement debt under section 17 of the Judgements Act 1838 and is to be regarded for enforcement purposes as part of the amount to be recovered from the defendant under the confiscation order (DTA 1994, s 10).

Although a confiscation order is enforced in a magistrates' court in the same way as any other Crown Court fine, subject to the above modifications, a cautious approach is required. Unlike other outstanding sums, the prosecution may itself take enforcement steps. A prosecutor may apply to the High Court in given circumstances for a restraining order, prohibiting any person from dealing with any realisable property, when a receiver may be appointed and for a charging order. Such action is quite separate and apart form any enforcement action taken in a magistrates' court and any proceedings a justices' clerk may himself take in the High Court. In view of this, it is suggested that before enforcement action is taken in the magistrates' court, there should be liaison with the prosecution.

2. Application of sums received

Under section 30 of the DTA 1994 a justices' clerk receiving a payment on account of an amount payable under a confiscation order must reduce the amount payable under the order by the amount paid but must apply the money received in a given way. The justices' clerk must first pay any expenses incurred by a person acting as an insolvency practitioner and not already paid by any receiver. Also where the money has been paid to the justices' clerk by a receiver appointed for the purpose of drug trafficking proceedings, or in pursuance of a charging order, the justices' clerk must next pay the receiver's remuneration and expenses. The justices' clerk is then required to reimburse the prosecution for sums paid to a receiver (as well as any other person on whose application a receiver was appointed where proceedings for a drug trafficking offence are not instituted (DTA 1994, s 36(2))).

The way in which a justices' clerk's accounts are credited will mean that when a payment is made to a justices' clerk, the full amount received operates to reduce the amount of the confiscation order proportionately. However an adjustment must be shown in his accounts to show that not all of the sum is necessarily paid to the Lord Chancellor's Department as if it were a fine because of the deductions which first have to be made as set out above.

Because of the need to make payments in a given order to reimburse receivers etc. for expenses incurred, it is incumbent upon justices' clerks when payments are made to discharge confiscation orders, to make inquiry of the prosecution.

3. Imprisonment

Where default is made in payment of a confiscation order and imprisonment for default has been imposed by the Crown Court, the commitment warrant falls to be issued. A hearing must be held at which the defendant is given the opportunity to make representations and to put forward reasons why the warrant should not be issued. At the time the confiscation order was made, the Crown Court will have assessed the value of any assets available to satisfy the outstanding sum (see above). The defendant may argue that any property is no longer capable of realising the value originally fixed (and, with the recent downturn in the property market, this is likely to be much more common) and that the reason for the failure to pay is due to the lower value of the asset. In such a case the defendant should be given the opportunity to apply to the High Court for a certificate enabling him to apply to the Crown Court for a variation of confiscation order.

Other powers to make confiscation orders

1. Power to make orders

Section 71 of the CJA 1988, gives Crown Courts and magistrates' courts power to make confiscation orders in cases other than drug trafficking, requiring an offender to pay such sum as the court thinks fit. Where a person is convicted in the Crown Court of an indictable offence which is not a drug trafficking offence, or is convicted by the Crown Court or a magistrates' court of an offence listed in Schedule 4 of the 1988 Act (offences concerning sex establishments; supplying video recordings of unclassified work, or possessing for the purposes of supply; use of unlicensed premises for exhibition which require a licence; (acid house) parties; and offences infringing copyright and the use of trademarks) a confiscation order can be made. Before an order is made by a magistrates' court the court must be satisfied that an individual has benefited from the offence or from an offence taken together with some other scheduled offence of which he is convicted in the same proceedings, or which the court takes into consideration in determining sentence; and that he has benefited at least to the minimum amount (which is £10,000 or such other amount as the Secretary of State may specify by order made by statutory instrument. Where a person has so benefited, then in addition to dealing with the offender in any other way, a confiscation order may be made for the sum to be paid. The power to make an order is discretionary but cannot be exercised except on application by the prosecutor giving written notice to the court to the effect that it appears to him that, were the court to consider that it ought to make an order, it would be able to make an order requiring the offender to pay at least the minimum amount. The method of determining the amount of the order is set out in section 72 of the CJA 1988.

For the purposes of the Act, a person is treated as having benefited from an offence if he obtains property or a pecuniary advantage as a result of or in connection with the commission of the offence. The benefit is then the value of the property or pecuniary advantage so obtained. Unlike drug trafficking cases, the court has a discretion whether to make an order and is not duty bound to do so.

Where the court makes both a confiscation order and at the same time makes an order for the payment of compensation, and it appears that the defendant will not have sufficient means to satisfy both orders in full, the court must direct that the compensation is paid out of any sums received (CJA 1988, s 72(7)).

2. Enforcement

Subject to the modification below, a confiscation order made by the Crown Court is collected and enforced in a magistrates' court as if it were a fine imposed by the Crown Court recoverable in a magistrates' court. A confiscation order made by a magistrates' court is enforced as if it were a fine imposed by that court (CJA 1988, s 75).

As with confiscation orders in drug trafficking cases, a commitment warrant issued by a magistrates' court must run consecutively with any period of imprisonment, youth custody or detention which the accused is liable to serve in respect of the original offence, including any period of imprisonment or detention in default of payment of a fine for the offence imposed by the Crown Court, except where the warrant of commitment has not been issued (CJA 1988, s 75(4)).

An amount ordered to be paid by way of a confiscation order may not be remitted as if it were a fine. The defendant may however apply to the High Court for a certificate that realisable property is inadequate for the purpose of the amount to be recovered under the order. Once the certificate has been given he may then apply to the court which made the order for the amount to be reduced.

In the case of persons aged under 18, the court cannot make an order requiring a parent or guardian to enter a recognisance to ensure payment or directing a parent or guardian to pay the balance of the outstanding sum (CJA 1988, s 75(5)).

Where a justices' clerk wishes to take proceedings in the High Court or county court to recover the outstanding sum, a means inquiry is not required to authorise such proceedings (CJA 1988, s 75(5)(*b*)).

As with drug trafficking offences, the prosecutor may take proceedings in the High Court for a restraining order or a charging order.

3. Application of sums received

Sums in the hands of a receiver appointed in proceedings taken by the prosecutor are applied first in payment of expenses incurred (if any) by an insolvency practitioner (defined in section 388 of the IA 1986); then to such payment if any as the High Court may direct; and thereafter in satisfaction of the debt.

Where a justices' clerk receives a sum in payment of the outstanding debt, he must apply the sums received in a given order. First the justices' clerk must pay out of the sums received any expenses incurred by a person acting as an insolvency practitioner who has not already been paid. If money has been paid to a justices' clerk by a receiver appointed in confiscation proceedings, or in pursuance of a charging order, the clerk must next pay the receiver's remuneration and expenses. After making these payments the Clerk is next then required to reimburse any amount paid by a prosecutor to a receiver or to any other person on whose application the receiver was appointed where proceedings for an offence have not been instituted (CJA 1988, s 81).

It is the full amount received by the justices' clerk which is taken to reduce the amount of the outstanding liability. The deductions as set out above must then be made and the balance forwarded to the Secretary of State.

A further complexity which is introduced occurs when a sum recovered under a confiscation order is to be applied first in payment of a compensation order as well as remuneration and expenses. The person entitled to the compensation (the compensatee) is liable to pay a contribution out of the compensation towards the remuneration or expenses in the same proportion as the total amount of the compensation bears to the total amount of the compensation order. The justices' clerk is then required to deduct this amount from the compensation which would otherwise be paid to the compensatee, and the compensatee is treated as having received the full amount due.

Bankruptcy

Enforcement against persons adjudged bankrupt or against whom bankruptcy proceedings have been instituted has presented courts with some difficulty. However the position is relatively straightforward and need not be regarded as one of unusual complexity.

1. Payments void

Where a person is adjudged bankrupt any disposition of property (which includes payment by cash) is void without the consent of the bankruptcy court, if made during the period beginning with the day of the presentation of the petition for bankruptcy and ending with the vesting of the bankrupt's estate in the trustee.

Payments made to clear fines etc. made during this period would therefore seem to be void (IA 1986, s 234).

2. Staying enforcement proceedings

At any time when bankruptcy proceedings are pending or an individual has been adjudged bankrupt, the bankruptcy court may stay any action or other legal process against the property or person of the bankrupt (IA 1986, s 285(1)). This includes staying proceedings before magistrates. In *Smith* v *Braintree District Council* [1989] 3 All ER 897, the House of Lords decided that the words "other legal process" were to be construed to protect the bankrupt's estate from all creditors. An order made by the county court on the application of the debtor to stay committal proceedings before magistrates for non-payment of rates was upheld. The case would appear to be sufficiently wide enough to apply equally to the fines, community charge and council tax cases.

Notwithstanding this power, jurisdiction to stay enforcement proceedings appears to be given to a magistrates' court itself. By section 285(2) of the IA 1986, any court in which proceedings are pending against an individual may, on proof that a bankruptcy petition has been presented in respect of that individual or that he is an undischarged bankrupt, either stay the proceedings or allow them to continue on such terms as it thinks fit.

3. Recovery of fines etc

A fine is not a debt provable in bankruptcy so that it is not open to lodge in bankruptcy for payment or part-payment of the outstanding amount (Insolvency Rules 1986, r 12). The word "fine" has the same meaning as in the MCA 1980 i.e. "... includes any pecuniary penalty or pecuniary forfeiture or pecuniary compensation payable under a conviction". This would appear to exclude compensation ordered under section 35 of the PCCA 1973, which is enforced as a sum adjudged to be paid by conviction and not as a fine (Administration of Justice Act 1970, s 41). A forfeited recognisance however, is enforced as a fine and would appear to fall within the definition (MCA 1980, s 120(4)), although costs awarded on conviction do not. Furthermore any obligation arising under a confiscation order made under section 1 of the Drug Trafficking Offences Act 1988 is not provable in bankruptcy.

4. Discharge and further liability

The discharge of a bankrupt does not release him from all liability in respect of a fine imposed for an offence or from any liability under a recognisance (except in the case of offences under enactments relating to public revenue or of a recognisance with the consent of the Treasury (IA 1986, s 281(4))). On the discharge of a bankrupt it is possible to bring proceedings for the recovery of fines which have been held in suspense during the bankruptcy and to recover amounts which were not provable.

5. Administration orders

Section 112 of the County Courts Act 1984 gives to the county court power to make an administration order against a debtor "where a debtor is unable to pay forthwith the amount of any debt owed by him." The order may be made on the application of the debtor, any creditor or of the court's own motion.

The question arises whether a fine can be made the subject of an administration order. Although the position is not entirely free from ambiguity, and there are differing views, one persuasive view is that a fine cannot be made the subject of an administration order, the reason for which appears to be based upon the comments of Hobhouse LJ in *Preston BC* v *Riley and Riley* (1995), *The Times,* 19 April when referring to Part VI of the County Court Act 1984 he said that "In my judgement it is the bankruptcy legislation which provides the context in which the provision of Part VI (administration orders) have to be construed".

As a fine is not provable in bankruptcy (see above) Hobhouse LJ's comments would seem to lead to the conclusion that a fine cannot therefore be made the subject of an administration order.

CHAPTER 6

Recovery of Fines by Deduction from Income Support

CHAPTER 6

Recovery of Fines by Deduction from Income Support

Introduction

Section 24 of the Criminal Justice Act 1991 made provision for the first time for the recovery of fines by deductions from income support. The reference to a fine in that section includes not only a fine imposed on an offender by a magistrates' court but also an amount ordered to be paid by way of costs which is treated as having been adjudged to be paid on a conviction by a magistrates' court by virtue of the provisions of section 41 of the Administration of Justice Act 1970. This includes costs awarded by the Crown Court, Court of Appeal (Criminal Division) or the House of Lords and also an amount imposed by way of penalty under the Vehicle Excise and Registration Act 1994 and the Customs and Excise Management Act 1979 and any amount ordered to be paid by way of additional duty under the Vehicle Excise and Registration Act 1994. An amount ordered to be paid by way of compensation may also be deducted from income support. Deductions can be made where the offender is entitled to income support within the meaning of the Social Security Act 1986 either alone or together with any unemployment, sickness or invalidity benefit, retirement pension or severe disablement allowance which is paid by means of the same instrument. The statute does not make provision for the enforcement of legal aid contribution orders be recovered by this method.

The Fines (Deductions from Income Support) Regulations 1992 made under section 24 of the Criminal Justice Act 1991 now provide for deductions to be made in the circumstances prescribed by the statute.

Applications for deductions from income support

The Regulations provide for the court to make application to the Secretary of State to ask him to deduct sums from any amounts payable to an offender by way of income support. However before making such an application the court is required to hold a means inquiry. The application to the Secretary of State is required to be made in the form set out in

Schedule 3 to the Regulations, or one to like effect (see below). The application, whether made in the form shown or on one similar to it must contain the following information:

1. the offender's name and address, and if it is known his date of birth;
2. the date when the fine was imposed or the compensation order made;
3. the name and address of the court imposing the fine or compensation order;
4. the amount of the fine or compensation order;
5. the date on which the application is made;
6. the date on which the means inquiry was held;
7. whether the offender has defaulted in paying the fine or compensation order.

The application is made when it is sent or delivered to a Social Security office and where insufficient information is given then the Secretary of State may require the court to furnish such further information as may reasonably be required to enable the offender to be identified.

Deductions from offender's income support

Where an application is received it is referred to an adjudication officer who determines whether there is sufficient entitlement to income support to enable a deduction to be made. The determination should be made so far as practicable within 14 days of receipt of the reference from the Secretary of State. The Secretary of State is then required to notify the court in writing again so far as is practicable within 14 days from the date he receives the decision from the adjudication officer. At the same time the Secretary of State notifies the offender of his right to appeal.

Where the adjudication officer has determined that there is sufficient entitlement to income support the Secretary of State may deduct a sum equal to 5% of the personal allowance for a single claimant aged not less than 25 years old.

Deductions will only be made where the offender is entitled to income support throughout any benefit week and no deductions are being made in respect of him under any other application. Deductions will not be made unless the offender at the date of the application by the court is aged not less than 18 years old and he is entitled to income support and he has defaulted in paying the fine. Deductions are made when income

Application to Secretary of State under the Fines (Deductions from Income Support) Regulations 1992

To: Department of Social Security
[insert address of appropriate office]

Date:

Particulars of Offender

Name:

Address:

Date of Birth:

The court applies to the Secretary of State in respect of each of the fines and compensation orders listed in column 1 below, imposed on the above-named offender by the court on the dates specified in column 2 below against the fine or compensation order specified in column 1. In respect of each order, the court asks the Secretary of State to deduct sums from any amount payable to the offender by way of income support to secure the payment of the amount shown in column 4 below.

The offender is/is not in default and the court has inquired on [ ] into the offender's means.

1 **Description of penalty imposed**	2 **Date imposed**	3 **Amount imposed** **£**	4 **Amount sought to be recovered by deduction** **£**	**£**
			Total amount sought to be recovered by deduction	

By order of the Court –

Clerk of the Court

[ ] Court

ADDRESS

support is paid to the offender. Deductions will not be made if there is no longer sufficient entitlement to income support or the entitlement to income support ceases altogether; or the court withdraws its application for deductions to be made or the liability to make payment ceases.

Where further applications for deductions are made, the Secretary of State refers the further applications to the adjudication officer one at a time and in date order; the date of the application being the relevant date for these purposes.

Although deductions are made as each payment of income support is made to the offender; payments of sums deducted from income support are made to the court at intervals of 13 weeks.

The court is under a duty to inform the Secretary of State within 21 days when the whole of the amount to which the application relates has been paid. The Secretary of State is obliged to notify the offender in writing of the total of sums deducted under any application following a written request to that effect from the offender or when the deductions have ceased.

The court may withdraw an application at any time by giving notice in writing to the Social Security office to which the application was sent or delivered.

Appeal

An offender may appeal against the determination of the adjudication officer to a tribunal, and from there the offender or the adjudication officer may appeal to a commissioner but only where it is said that the tribunal's decision was erroneous in point of law. Where an appeal falling to be heard by one of the commissioners involves a question of law of special difficulty, the Chief Commissioner may direct that the appeal be dealt with not by that commissioner alone, but by a tribunal consisting of any three of the commissioners. An appeal from the commissioner on a question of law may be made by the offender, the adjudication officer or the Secretary of State. The regulations also make provision for leave to be granted before an appeal is heard. Ultimately an appeal may be made to the Court of Appeal in England and Wales or the Court of Session in Scotland.

Review, correction of accidental errors and setting aside decisions

Any decision of an adjudication officer, a tribunal or a commissioner may be reviewed at any time by an adjudication officer where the officer is satisfied that the decision was given in ignorance of, or was based on a mistake, some material fact or there has been change of circumstances since the decision was given.

Any decision of an adjudication officer may be reviewed by another adjudication officer on the grounds that the decision was erroneous on point of law.

An application to review is made in writing to the adjudication officer, stating the grounds of the application. The adjudication officer is required to consider the grounds and, so far as is practicable, dispose of the application within 14 days of its receipt. A decision given by way of revision or a refusal to review is subject to appeal in the same manner as the original decision.

Provision is made for accidental errors to be corrected by the person or tribunal by whom the decision was made and to be deemed to be part of the decision or the record of that decision.

There is also provision in the regulations to set aside decisions on certain grounds. This includes a decision made by an adjudication officer, a tribunal or a commissioner or a determination given on an application for leave to appeal and provides that the decision may be set aside by the adjudicating authority which gave the decision where it appears just to set that decision aside on the grounds that:

1. a document relating to the proceedings in which the decision was given was not sent to, or was not received at an appropriate time by a party to the proceedings or the party's representative or was not received at the appropriate time by the person or tribunal who gave that decision;
2. in the case of an appeal to a tribunal or an oral hearing before a Commissioner a party to the proceedings in which the decision was given or the party's representative was not present at the hearing relating to the proceedings; or
3. the interest of justice so requires.

Where an application is set aside every party to the proceedings must be given a reasonable opportunity to make representations before the application is determined. Once the application to set aside a decision has been determined every party must receive a notice, which must contain a statement giving the reasons for the determination, in writing as soon as is practicable.

Any application or appeal must be in writing and must be made or given by sending or delivering it to the appropriate office within the specified time. The time limits for making applications or appeals are detailed in Schedule 1 to the Regulations. An application for an extension of time may also be made under the Regulations except once it has been refused, it may not be renewed unless it is made to a Commissioner. The conduct and procedure in relation to any application or appeal is detailed in Schedule 2 to the Regulations. There are also special provisions for the service of notices under the Regulations.

There is no right of appeal against a correction of an accidental error or a refusal to make such a correction or a determination to set aside a decision.

Deductions from income support and committal to prison

Where the court exercises its power to require the Secretary of State to make deductions from income support and the adjudicator is satisfied that there is sufficient entitlement to income support, then the deduction will be made amounting to £2.40 per week (at the time of going to print). This payment does not assume any priority; where there are other liabilities then payments towards those debts may be given precedence in circumstances where the court might feel payments towards its order should be met first. Nevertheless the court is required to consider making an order whereby sums are deducted from income support before imposing imprisonment in default. In *R* v *Alfreton Justices, ex parte Gratton* (1993), *The Times* 17 December the court held in relation to a committal order imposed for non-payment of community charge that where the defendant had offered to make a payment to be deducted from his income support, "that if the justices did not consider imposing a viable deduction before deciding to commit they were plainly wrong". However in *R* v *Felixstowe Justices and Ipswich Borough Council, ex parte Herridge* (1993) Rating Appeals 83, which again concerned an appeal against the issue of a commitment warrant for non-payment of community charge, the court held that it was not necessary in every case for the court to enquire whether there was an alternative procedure whereby the enforcement of the debt might be obtained, and when the court took the view that the defendant could pay £10 per week then an alternative remedy (i.e. deduction from income support) which would provide at best £2 per week was not an alternative. In the unreported case of *R* v *Newcastle under Lyme Justices, ex parte Massey,* also a case where justices ordered committal to prison for non-payment of community charge, Pill J confirmed that there were circumstances in which those in receipt of income support could be properly committed to prison. However he did say that deductions from income support might often be appropriate where the court was considering a low payment order.

PART 3: ENFORCEMENT OF FIXED PENALTIES

CHAPTER 7

Fixed Penalties

CHAPTER 7

Fixed Penalties

Introduction

On 1 October 1986, Part III of the Transport Act 1982 came into force, bringing with it a dramatic extension of the original 1960 fixed penalty system. The 1982 Act has now been replaced by the Road Traffic Offenders Act 1988 (RTOA 1988) which extended the scope of the fixed penalty scheme further. Covering a wide range of offences (with the exception of "causing" or "permitting" a vehicle to be used by another), the system provides for a relatively low-cost and simple method of penalising road traffic offenders. Since there is no prosecution or court hearing the theory is that both police forces and magistrates' courts benefit; and of course those motorists who do pay also benefit by paying less as a result of waiving their right to a court hearing.

Where the motorist does not pay the penalty or request a hearing before the end of the "suspended enforcement period" the police must take further action to enforce the ticket through their central ticket office (CTO). This is done by a system of "fine registration". The motorist's lack of response to a notice served upon him raises a presumption of guilt of the original fixed penalty offence, and the Act then provides for the offence to be registered in the defaulter's home court for enforcement as a fine without a court hearing. This of course represents a major and radical departure from the accepted judicial practice in this country, and, recognising that mistakes can occur, certain safeguards have been built into the system to allow a defendant to challenge payment of the penalty and so avoid the consequences of enforcement.

Registration of sums payable in default for enforcement as fines

1. Driver present

Where on the occasion of the offence a constable gives a fixed penalty notice to the person whom he believes to be the alleged offender and:

1. the recipient does not give notice requesting a hearing, and
2. the fixed penalty is not paid before the end of the suspended enforcement period,

a sum equal to the fixed penalty plus one-half of that amount may be registered for enforcement as a fine against the recipient of the notice (RTOA 1988, s 55(3)).

2. Driver not present

Where the fixed penalty notice has been affixed to a vehicle under section 62 of the RTOA 1988, if the penalty is not paid before the expiration of the suspended enforcement period and there is no request for a court hearing, the police may serve a "notice to owner" upon any person who appears to be the owner of the vehicle in question. If there is no response to that notice within 21 days and the fixed penalty still remains unpaid, then a sum equal to the fixed penalty, plus one half of the amount of that penalty may be registered for enforcement as a fine against the person to whom notice was sent (RTOA 1988, s 64(2)).

3. Procedure

The procedure for registration commences when the police issue a certificate known as a "fine registration certificate", which must be sent to the clerk to the justices for the petty sessions area in which the defaulter appears to reside (s 70 RTOA 1988).

The registration certificate must under section 70(5) of the Act:

1. give particulars of the offence to which the fixed penalty notice relates, namely:
   - the serial number and date, time and place of issue of the notice to owner, notice to hirer or fixed penalty (as the case may be);
   - the vehicle registration number;
   - the driver number;
   - the amount of the appropriate fixed penalty;
   - the sum to be registered in default of payment of the fixed penalty;
2. indicate whether registration is authorised under s 55(3) or 64(2) of the 1988 Act; and
3. state the name and last known address of the defaulter and the amount of the sum payable in default.

If the defaulter does not reside in that petty sessions area, then the clerk receiving the notice must cause the certificate to be forwarded on to the clerk to the justices for the petty sessions area (including Scotland) where the defendant does appear to reside (RTOA 1988, s 71). It should not be returned to the police force which issued the certificate or the fixed penalty clerk for that area.

On receipt of the registration certificate the clerk must register the sum for enforcement by entering it in the court register. Separate registers are kept for this purpose, although they are regarded as part of the main court register (RTOA 1988, s 71(2); Magistrates' Court Rules 1981, r 66(B)).

Notice is then required to be served on the defaulter at the address given in the certificate of registration, specifying the amount due and giving information about the offence and the authority for registration (RTOA 1988, s 71(6); Magistrates Court Rules 1981, r 111). In the case of limited companies, notice can be sent to either of the following addresses:

1. the company's registered or principal office; or
2. the address kept by the Driver and Vehicle Licensing Centre for the purpose of excise duty records.

See Form 159 in the Magistrates Courts (Forms) Rules 1981 for the prescribed form of notice to defaulter.

If the certificate relates to an endorsable offence the clerk of any court receiving the registration certificate must also inform the fixed penalty clerk holding the relevant driving licence that the sum has been registered (Reg 8 Fixed Penalty (Procedure) Regulations 1986, reg 8). See Form 158 in the Magistrates Courts (Forms) Rules 1981 for the prescribed notice to the fixed penalty clerk.

Note that for these purposes a "person" includes a body both corporate and unincorporate and it would be wrong for any justices' clerk to refuse registration on the basis that an unincorporate association had no legal personality despite the obvious and practical difficulties of enforcement against that "person" *(R* v *Croydon Justices, ex parte Chief Constable of Kent* (1989) 154 JP 118).

4. Effect of registration

On a fixed penalty being registered for enforcement it has effect as if the sum so registered were a fine imposed by that court on the conviction of the defaulter on the date of registration (RTOA 1988, s71(7)(8)). Accordingly, the provisions of the MCA 1980 relating to the enforcement of fines apply and the power to remit fines contained in section 85 of the MCA 1980 is specifically included.

Challenging fine registration

1. Statutory declarations

As stated earlier, it is inevitable that, with the many hundreds of thousands of tickets being issued, the system will occasionally falter and mistakes will occur. It is important therefore to appreciate that the law allows for the penalty to be challenged even after registration and before the full consequences of enforcement arise. Where the fixed penalty was registered by virtue of section 55(3) of the RTOA 1988 (driver present) the person who has received notice of the registration may invalidate it under section 73(3) of the Act by making a statutory declaration to the effect that:

1. he was not the person to whom the relevant fixed penalty notice was given; or
2. that he gave notice requesting a hearing in respect of the alleged offence as permitted by the fixed penalty notice *before* the end of the suspended enforcement period.

See Form 160 in the Magistrates Courts (Forms) Rules 1981 for the prescribed form of statutory declaration.

Where the registration was made by virtue of section 64(2) of the RTOA 1988 (driver not present) the person who has received notice of the registration may invalidate it by making a statutory declaration to the effect that:

1. he did not know of the fixed penalty notice concerned or of any fixed penalty notice or notice to owner relating to that penalty until he received notice of the registration; or
2. he was not the owner of the vehicle at the time of the alleged offence, and he has a reasonable excuse for failing to comply with the notice to owner; or
3. he gave notice requesting a hearing before the end of the period allowed for response to the notice of owner

Form 161 in the Magistrates Courts (Forms) Rules 1981 is the prescribed form of statutory declaration.

The declaration must be made within 21 days of receiving notice of the registration, or of notice of any enforcement proceedings in respect of that registration, whichever is the earlier. It must be served on the clerk of the court which registered the sum either by delivering it to him, leaving it at his office or by sending it by registered post or recorded delivery to his office. It is possible for a single justice to extend the time limit for making a statutory declaration in cases where the justice considers there to be reasonable grounds for delay (RTOA 1988, s 74(2)).

2. Effect of a statutory declaration

On receiving a statutory declaration the clerk should scrutinise it for error. If there is none, he must accept it and cancel the fine registration and any endorsement made on the driving licence of the person making the declaration (RTOA 1988, ss 72(3)(4) and 73(3)). If any error is found he should contact the declarant. It should always be pointed out to the declarant that any person who knowingly and wilfully makes a statutory declaration which is false in a material particular is guilty of an offence and liable on conviction to imprisonment or a fine, or both (Perjury Act 1911, s 5).

A copy of the statutory declaration must be sent to the appropriate chief officer of police immediately, so that he can consider what further action is necessary (MCR 1981, r 112).

Conditional offers of fixed penalty

The RTOA 1988 extended the 1982 fixed penalty system even further by introducing a concept known as "conditional offer". In brief, if the police had reason to believe that a fixed penalty offence had been committed, but no fixed penalty under either section 54 or 62 of the 1988 Act had been issued, it could issue a conditional offer to pay the fixed penalty (and surrender the driving licence if endorsable) or be prosecuted through the court process. Because the liability to conviction of the offence is only discharged on payment of the fixed penalty, no other financial enforcement process arises. For further information on conditional offers see sections 75–77 of the RTOA 1988.

PART 4: ENFORCEMENT OF MAINTENANCE

CHAPTER 8

General Provisions Relating to the Enforcement of Maintenance Orders

CHAPTER 8

General Provisions Relating to the Enforcement of Maintenance Orders

Introduction

"A maintenance order" means any order specified in Schedule 8 to the Administration of Justice Act 1970, i.e. an order:

1. for alimony, maintenance or other payments made, or having effect as if made, under Part II of the Matrimonial Causes Act 1973 (financial relief for parties to marriage and children of family);
2. for payments to, or in respect of, a child, being an order made, or having effect as if made, under Part III of the 1973 Act (maintenance of children following divorce, etc);
3. for periodical or other payments made, or having effect as if made, under Part II of the 1973 Act;
4. for maintenance or other payments to, or in respect of a spouse or child, being an order made under Part I of the Domestic Proceedings and Magistrates' Courts Act 1978;
5. for periodical or other payments made or having effect as if made under Schedule 1 to the Children Act 1989.
6. either:
   (a) made or having effect as if made under paragraph 23 of Schedule 2 to the Children Act 1989; or
   (b) made under section 23 of the Ministry of Social Security Act 1966, section 18 of the Supplementary Benefits Act 1976, section 24 of the Social Security Act 1986 or section 106 of the Social Security Administration Act 1992 (various provisions for obtaining contributions from a person whose dependants are assisted or maintained out of public funds);
7. under section 43 of the National Assistance Act 1948 (recovery of costs of maintaining assisted person);
8. to which section 16 of the Maintenance Orders Act 1950 applies by virtue of subsection (2)(*b*) or (*c*) of that section, ie an order made by a court in Scotland or Northern Ireland and corresponding to one of those specified in the foregoing

paragraphs) and which has been registered in a court in England and Wales under Part II of that Act;

9. for maintenance within the meaning of the Maintenance Orders (Facilities and Enforcement) Act 1920 (Commonwealth orders enforceable in the United Kingdom) registered in, or confirmed by, a court in England and Wales under that Act;
10. for periodical or other payments made under Part I of the Matrimonial Proceedings and Property Act 1970;
11. for maintenance within the meaning of Part I of the Maintenance Orders (Reciprocal Enforcement) Act 1972 registered in a magistrates' court under the said Part I;
12. for maintenance within the meaning of Part I of the Civil Jurisdiction and Judgments Act 1982 which is registered in a magistrates' court under that Part;
13. for periodical or other payments made under Part III of the Matrimonial and Family Proceedings Act 1984.

All the above orders are either "maintenance orders" able to be made by a magistrates' court or are orders "enforceable as a magistrates' court maintenance order" in the magistrates' court (MCA 1980, s 150). The MCA 1980 and the Magistrates' Courts Rules 1981 prescribe most of the procedures for the enforcement of such orders, but before dealing with these it is worth discussing other factors which may affect the enforcement of a maintenance order.

Factors which may affect the enforcement of a maintenance order

1. Bankruptcy

Maintenance arrears are not recoverable in bankruptcy as the value of the debt is "incapable of being fairly estimated" within the requirements of bankruptcy law. Nevertheless, proceedings may still be taken for enforcement against a person who is bankrupt or subject to bankruptcy proceedings (*James* v *James* [1963] 2 All ER 465).

2. Death

If either the person liable to make payments, or the person entitled to receive payments dies, the general position is that the order, together with the power to enforce, will cease.

Arrears owing to a party at the time of that party's death cannot be recovered in a magistrates' court by the party's legal representative, but any moneys in the possession of the court collecting officer at the time of death are part of the deceased's estate (*Re Green (A Bankrupt), ex parte Official Receiver* v *Cutting* [1979] 1 All ER 832). Arrears owed by a defendant who dies cannot be recovered against his estate (*Re Bidie, Bidie* v *General Accident Fire and Life Assurance Corporation Ltd* [1948] 2 All ER 995). No authority exists about the effect of death upon an order expressed to be paid direct to a child (as opposed to the mother for the child's benefit), or an order expressed to be paid through a third party. It is submitted, however, that death of the complainant does not terminate an order under which money is paid direct to a child because of the personal nature of the order between the payer and the child. Similarly, it is submitted that an order for payment through a third party will not lapse upon the death of the original complainant. (See also 151 JPN 160.)

3. Dissolution of marriage and remarriage

A marriage which has been dissolved since the making of the maintenance order does not prevent the order from being enforced (*Wood* v *Wood* [1957] 2 All ER 14). Likewise an order may be enforced even though the party to whom the arrears are due has remarried.

4. Discharge

Where an order has been discharged it remains a maintenance order for the purpose of enforcement provided there are still arrears to be recovered (MCA 1980, s 150).

5. Repealed legislation

A maintenance order made under legislation which has since been repealed remains a maintenance order for the purposes of payment and enforcement provided the order has not expired and/or arrears are outstanding.

6. Appeal

There is nothing to prevent an order being enforced pending an appeal, though generally it would be quite wrong to do so. In *Kendal* v *Wilkinson* (1855) 19 JP 467. Lord Campbell CJ said:

> *"In the vast majority of cases it would be exceedingly improper for a justice to grant a warrant after the notice ... and before the hearing of the appeal ..., but I do not think that in granting it he could be said to have acted without jurisdiction."*

Lord Campbell remarked on the inequity that would arise where the defendant, never intending to prosecute the appeal, could "as a matter of right entirely escape all liability to contribute".

Kendal v *Wilkinson* establishes the principle (confirmed in *R* v *Wilmot* [1861]) that, while it is lawful to enforce the order pending an appeal against it, it would be improper where the appeal is bona fide. This is difficult to reconcile with *R* v *Durham Justices* (1891) 55 JP 277 in which it was held that the court to which the appeal was being made is the exclusive judge of the sufficiency of the grounds. Quite clearly, there would have to be "exceptional" circumstances before the order was enforced. However, that does not mean that the clerk is entitled to withhold money from the other party pending an appeal. In *Board* v *Board* [1981] 11 Fam Law 210 Holin J said "that the bringing of an appeal did not operate as a stay on the proceedings", and the clerk was wrong in withholding money from the appellant's wife.

7. Validity

Where there has been no appeal or where an appeal has been unsuccessful, the court may not concern itself with the validity of the order to be enforced *(Sammy-Joe* v *GPO Mount Pleasant Office and Another* [1966] 3 All ER 924).

8. Imprisonment

Imprisonment or other detention for failing to pay maintenance arrears does not discharge the defendant from his liability to pay. He cannot, however, be imprisoned or detained a second time for the same arrears (MCA 1980, s 93(8); Maintenance Order Act 1958, s 17).

9. Registration

An order registered in a magistrates' court is enforceable in that court and cannot be enforced, during the subsistence of registration, in the court which originally made it. This does not mean that enforcement proceedings can be taken only in the court of registration. It is neither the purpose of the Maintenance Order Act 1950 (MOA 1950) nor of the Maintenance Order Act 1958 (MOA 1958) to limit the hearing of enforcement proceedings to a single magistrates' court. The more fundamental purpose is to give magistrates' courts in England and Wales jurisdiction to entertain proceedings in relation to orders which they could not themselves have made. Registered orders can be enforced in all respects as if they had been made by the court of registration, and consequently rule 59 of the Magistrates' Courts Rules 1981 will apply, allowing proceedings to be heard elsewhere than in the court of registration (MOA 1950, s 18(6); MOA 1958, s 3(4)).

10. Further proceedings

Proceedings can be taken to enforce payment of a sum due and unpaid under a maintenance order notwithstanding that a previous complaint has been made in respect of that sum, or a part thereof, and whether or not an order was made in those previous proceedings (MOA 1958, s 20(8)).

Procedures for enforcement

1. The court collecting officer

Until 1914, the responsibility for enforcing a maintenance order lay with the claimant. The Affiliation Orders Act 1914 gave justices a discretion to direct that maintenance payments be made through a third party (usually the justices' clerk), thus abolishing the necessity for the claimant to have any further communication with the payer. In 1935 these arrangements were revised and extended. The present position is that a "justice's clerk is, by virtue of his office, collecting officer of any magistrates' court of which he is clerk". However, the clerk is not the justices' agent when he receives payments in his capacity as court collecting officer (*O'Connor* v *Isaacs* [1956] 2 All ER 417).

As collecting officer, a justices' clerk has a duty to discharge all functions that are conferred on him by enactments relating to the collection, payment and enforcement of maintenance.

2. Notification of arrears

Where an order requires periodical payments to be made to the magistrates' court clerk and the payments are at any time in arrears to an amount equal to four times the weekly sum (or, in the case of payments to be made monthly or less frequently, twice the sum payable periodically), the clerk must give written particulars of the arrears to the person entitled to receive them, unless it appears to the clerk unnecessary or inexpedient to do so (Magistrates' Court Rules 1981, r 40). While the rules provide for notice to be given only once, in practice most courts will do this on a more regular basis, and indeed many accounting systems, particularly computerised, provide a continuous update of information.

Previous rules provided that special circumstances were required before the clerk could exercise his discretion not to give notice. Accordingly, it used to be said that regular appearances at the clerk's office by the person to whom notice was to be given were not special as in fact they were an everyday occurrence. The rules no longer require special circumstances and it is therefore submitted that it would be unnecessary to give notice where a person regularly calls at the clerk's office and is kept fully informed of the arrears position.

No form of notice is prescribed by the rules.

3. Penalty for breaching method of payment

Section 2 of the Maintenance Enforcement Act 1991 made it mandatory for magistrates' courts to order that maintenance payments be made by one of four methods:

- direct to creditor
- to the court
- by standing order or
- by attachment of earnings order.

Section 3 of the Act creates a new section 59B to the Magistrates' Courts Act 1980 and provides a sanction in the event that a person ordered to pay maintenance by a particular method does not comply with that part of the order. The sanction is the power to order the debtor to pay a sum not exceeding £1000. Process is by complaint being made by the creditor and a summons issued to the debtor. Any sum ordered to be paid is to be treated as a fine and not part of the maintenance order.

4. The complaint for arrears

Proceedings are begun by complaint. In establishing the amount of arrears due under each order (excluding lump sums), the provisions contained in rule 60(2) of the Magistrates' Courts Rules 1981 relating to apportionment should be considered. Where periodical payments are being made by one person to another person under more than one order, then proceedings for enforcement may be brought using only one complaint, provided the complaint indicates the payments that are due under each order (MCA 1980, s 93(1)).

No form of complaint is now prescribed; the Affiliation Proceedings Act 1957, which preserved the Bastardy (Forms) Order 1915, was repealed by the Family Law Reform Act 1987.

The complaint can be made to either a Justice of the Peace or, if not, on oath, to a justices' clerk (see Justices' Clerks Rules 1970), by:

1. the person entitled to payments, including, in the case of a child, the person with whom the child has his home (MCA 1980, s 62(1)); or
2. the justices' clerk (where the order requires payments through the court or by standing authority) if requested or authorised to do so in writing by the person for whose benefit the payments are required (MCA (1980), s 59A).

In the latter case, the clerk must take proceedings unless it appears to him to be unreasonable in the circumstances to do so. A refusal by the clerk to act in his own name will not prevent the person entitled to payments from taking proceedings on his own account. In practice, however, the first action will usually come from the clerk who will request from the person entitled to payment an "authority to enforce". Surprisingly, this is not always forthcoming. If the clerk does take proceedings in his own name the liability for costs properly incurred in the proceedings falls on the person requesting the clerk as if he had made the complaint himself. Authority to enforce may be cancelled, by the person for whose benefit the payments are required to be made, at any time by giving notice in writing to the clerk of a relevant court (MCA 1980, s 59A(4)).

5. Jurisdiction

Rule 59(1) of the Magistrates' Court Rules 1981 provides that a complaint for the enforcement of a magistrates' maintenance order, or an order enforceable as a magistrates' court maintenance order, must be heard by the court that made the order. There are two exceptions to this rule:

1. Where
- the complainant is the person in whose favour the order was made or, if that person is a child, the child or the person with whom the child had his home, and
- the complainant resides in a petty sessions area other than that for which the court acts, and payment is directed to be made either to the complainant or the magistrates' court clerk acting for the petty sessions area,
- the complaint can then be heard by the last-mentioned court;
2. where the complainant is the magistrates' court clerk, the complaint may be heard by that court.

6. Transfer of proceedings

Where a complaint is made to a Justice of the Peace for the enforcement of a magistrates' court maintenance order (including a registered order) and it appears to him that the defendant is for the time being in some other petty sessions area and that the order may be more conveniently enforced by a magistrates' court acting for that area, the justice shall cause the clerk of the court ("the administering court") to send the complaint by post to the clerk for that other area (Magistrates' Court Rules 1981, r 59(2)). Any information likely to assist the other court in its proceedings should also accompany the complaint. A complaint not on oath may be made to a justices' clerk who may also determine the venue.

On receipt of the complaint the other court must issue either a summons or, if the complaint purports to be on oath, a warrant for procuring the appearance of the defendant before it. It may then hear and determine the complaint (Magistrates' Court Rules 1981, r 59(3)).

If money is received under the order after the complaint has been sent to the other court, the clerk of the court receiving payment must immediately send a certificate stating the date and the amount of the payment. Similarly, if any payments are made direct to the person entitled to receive payments, that person must forthwith inform the clerk to whom the complaint was originally made in order that he may inform the clerk of the court subsequently dealing with the matter. Rule 59(6) of Magistrates' Court Rules 1981 provides that any certificate issued under this procedure and signed by the clerk of the court to whom the complaint was originally made is admissible as evidence of the amount specified and date of payment specified. It is submitted, however, that unless there is strong evidence to the contrary, the other court should always treat any certified payment as having been appropriated to the arrears and nothing else. No form of certificate of payment is prescribed by the rules.

In deciding whether to transfer proceedings, it need only appear to the administering court that the defendant "is for the time being" in some other area, and not that the defendant resides there. Furthermore, as it is the administering court which determines that the order may be more conveniently enforced by another magistrates' court, there appears to be no way in which the other court can refuse to act.

In practice, however, if the administering court becomes aware that the defendant is in yet another court area, or even back within its own jurisdiction, it will seek to withdraw proceedings from the transferred venue and start again. Similarly, if attempts by the other court to trace the defendant are unsuccessful the other court will usually return the complaint giving the original court such information as it has managed to ascertain about the defendant's whereabouts.

Where any decision is reached, or warrant of distress or commitment is issued, in pursuance of a complaint relating to the enforcement of a maintenance order, being a complaint heard by a court other than the administering court, then the clerk of that court must immediately send to the clerk of the administering court an extract from the court register containing the decision. On receipt of that extract the clerk of the administering court must enter the particulars in his court register (Magistrates' Courts (Maintenance Orders Act 1958) Rules 1959, r 21). Form 154 in the Magistrates' Courts (Forms) Rules 1981 is the prescribed form of extract from register proving proceedings of a magistrates' court.

7. Summons and warrant

Once a complaint has been laid, invariably a summons will be issued directing the defaulter to appear before the court. However, if the complaint has been substantiated on oath, a warrant without bail may be issued for the defendant's arrest whether or not a summons has previously been issued (MCA 1980, s 93(5)). Despite this, a court should only issue a warrant in the first instance if satisfied that a summons would be ineffective. No form of summons or warrant is prescribed.

8. Time limits

Proceedings cannot be commenced earlier than the 15th day after the making of the order (MCA 1980, s 93(2)). Unlike civil debt, it is not necessary to serve a copy of the order on the defendant before it can be enforced. In practice, however, a copy of the order will have been served before proceedings began. From the 15th day after the making of the order onwards a complaint can be made at any time.

9. Payment and discharge of process

It is the practice of all courts to dispense with the defaulter's attendance if the amount due is paid, in full, before the return date. This practice derives from the wording of Form 18 of the Bastardy (Forms) Order 1915, as amended by the Bastardy (Forms) Order 1935, previously the appropriate form of warrant. The relevant words, "unless the said sum and all costs and charges be sooner paid", were in brackets and could be deleted if the justices thought fit. If the words were struck out the constable executing the warrant had no power to receive the amount due and had to bring the defaulter to court as directed by the warrant. In the case of a persistent defaulter who could afford to pay but was prepared to put the complainant, the court and the police to constant trouble, this was a useful way of ensuring that he could be told of the trouble he caused. The repeal of the Bastardy (Forms) Order 1935 leaves the continuance of this practice in some considerable doubt and it is submitted that payment of the whole debt discharges the debtor's obligation and his consequent arrest.

10. Tracing missing defendants

No amount of legislation will produce any money if the defendant cannot be found. As a last resort, certain government departments are prepared to assist in tracing missing defendants if information such as a National Insurance number or a photograph is supplied to them. If they are able to assist, any information is supplied on the strict understanding that it will be used only for the purpose of the proceedings and not supplied to anyone else. The procedure to be used is described in detail in Home Office Circular 140/1971 and Practice Direction [1973] 1 All ER 61. The addresses to which enquiries about former servicemen are to be sent are contained in Practice Direction [1979] 2 All ER 1106.

The hearing

1. Family Proceedings

Enforcement proceedings are not automatically family proceedings, but certain provisions applicable to family proceedings, such as the power to require a report on the parties' means, and the duty to assist an unrepresented party who is unable to examine or cross-examine a witness effectively, apply also to enforcement (MCA 1980, ss 72 and 73). The justices may, if they think fit, order that the proceedings be treated as family proceedings, in which case other provisions, such as reporting restrictions, can be applied (MCA 1980, s 65(2)). This practice is strongly recommended, as justices who are not family panel members are often ill-equipped to cope with the complexities of maintenance enforcement.

2. Proof of non-payment

Under section 99 of the MCA 1980, proof of non-payment may take either of the following forms, unless the court requires the clerk or other person to be called as a witness:

1. if the person to whom the sum is ordered to be paid is a magistrates' court clerk, a certificate purporting to be signed by the clerk that the sum has not been paid to him; and
2. in any other case a document purporting to be a statutory

declaration by the person to whom the sum was ordered to be paid that the sum has not been paid to him.

The certificate or declaration can, of course, be rebutted. The prescribed forms are Forms 146, 147 in the Magistrates' Courts (Forms) Rules 1981.

3. Means inquiry reports

In proceedings for the enforcement of a maintenance order made in "family proceedings" as defined in section 65(1) of the MCA 1980, the court can direct a probation officer to investigate the parties' means, and require him to provide the court with either a written report of his investigations or an oral statement (MCA 1980, s 72).

Where the court requires a written report, a copy must be given to each party to the proceedings or their legal representative. The court may, if it thinks fit, require the report (or such part of it as it specifies) to be read aloud at the hearing.

The court or either of the parties to the proceedings can require that the probation officer attend to give evidence about his investigations. Either party may give or call evidence regarding to any matter contained in the report or in the evidence given by the officer.

Both the officer's report and evidence can be received by the court, notwithstanding any provision that would otherwise make these matters inadmissible as evidence. This exception is indeed sensible, as most investigative reports rely heavily on hearsay and the court would otherwise be deprived of relevant and useful information. However, great care must be taken to distinguish statement of fact from statement of opinion.

4. Adjournments

Proceedings for enforcement can be adjourned, but the defendant cannot be remanded. The court can proceed in his absence if it is proved to the satisfaction of the court (on oath or in such manner as prescribed by rule 67 of the Magistrates' Court Rules 1981) that the summons was served within what appears to be a reasonable time before the hearing, or that the defendant has previously appeared (MCA 1980, s 93(3)). Appearances may be made by solicitor or counsel except, for example, where personal appearance is required by recognisance (MCA 1980, s 122).

If a complaint is substantiated on oath, a warrant may be issued, whether or not a summons has been issued previously.

5. Remission of arrears

On the hearing of a complaint for the enforcement of a magistrates' court maintenance order, the court can remit the whole or any part of the sum due under the order (MCA 1980, s 95). However, before doing so, the court must, unless it appears unnecessary or impracticable to do so, notify the person in whose favour the order was made and allow that person a reasonable opportunity to make representations to the court, either orally or in writing (Magistrates' Court Rules 1981, r 44). Any written representations may be considered by the court if they are purportedly signed by or on behalf of the person entitled to payments. No form of notice is prescribed by the rules. *Certiorari* will follow if rule 44 is not complied with (*R* v *Dover Magistrates' Court, ex parte Kidner* [1983] 1 All ER 475). This point was once again reaffirmed in A v A (Remission of Arrears: Procedure) [1996] 1 FCR 629.

No guidance is given of when it would be "unnecessary" or "impracticable" to give notice. Presumably where the court already has an agreement to the remission from the person entitled to payments then notice would be unnecessary. Other examples might include a long history of non-response by the person entitled to payment, or where the whereabouts of that person are no longer known. It is suggested, however, that any doubt should be resolved in favour of the person entitled to payment and the matter adjourned for notice to be given.

The rules are very clear as to whom notice is to be given. This does not include the State unless the order has been made in their favour.

The rules do not specify a specific form of notice, merely what the notice should contain. Experience has shown, however, that many people are not familiar with the word "remit" and, where possible, a simple form of explanation should be used.

"It will be a matter entirely for the magistrate's discretion on the light of the evidence before him whether to enforce or to remit as he thinks proper the whole or any part of the sum due . . . " (per Lord Meriman P, *Pilcher* v *Pilcher* (No 2) (1956) 120 JP 127). In exercising their discretion to remit, it has been said that justices should usually follow Family Division practice and enforce only arrears which have accrued within the year before the date of complaint. This is only a rule of practice, although it is usually followed. The court can consider whether, in the circumstances of any given case, it is right to follow the practice either in whole or in part. The practice was approved and followed in *Luscombe* v *Luscombe* [1962] 1 All ER 668 and *Freeman-Thomas* v *Freeman-Thomas* [1963] 1 All ER 17. In *Ross* v *Pearson* (1976) 140 JP 282 it was established that while the practice could be appropriately used in the magistrates' court, there was an absolute rule preventing the enforcement of arrears more than one year old. Thus, in *Russell* v *Russell* [1986] 1 FLR 465 it was held that the fact that a consent order had been made in the county court within 12 months of the complaint was a justifiable reason for distinguishing the case from the usual case where "stale arrears" were being considered. However, it was held in *Dickens* v *Pattison* (1985) 15 Fam Law 163 that the mere fact that the person liable to pay the maintenance was an irregular or reluctant payer was not an unusual circumstance, and did not justify departure from that normal rule. Sir John Donaldson MC in *Russell* v *Russell* said that justices who consider they have a "discretion to remit" are misdirecting themselves; the "discretion" is one to "enforce". This very point was restated by Johnson J in *B* v *C* [1995] 2 FCR 678.

Whilst the court has power to remit any sum due and unpaid at the date of complaint, it has no power to remit any sums already paid to the collecting officer and held by him (*Fildes (formerly Simkin)* v *Simkin* (1959) 124 JP 13).

The power to remit is clearly an exercise of the court's discretion, which like all discretions, must be exercised judicially and not capriciously. Therefore, remission of arrears due to a wife is not justified simply because she has impeded the defendant's right to have access to his children. Since maintenance payments are not a reward for allowing access, remission should not be imposed as a penalty for refusing it (see *R* v *Halifax Justices, ex parte Woolverton* (1979) 123 Sol Jo 80).

Appealing a decision of justices to remit arrears is by notice of motion to a Judge of the Family Division under section 94 of the Children Act 1989 in respect of an order made under that Act.

See later for other types of cases (S v S (1992) *The Times* 8 December).

It is an improper use of the justices' discretion to remit arrears to satisfy payment of a mother's debt where the maintenance payments are payable to and belong to the child (*Parry* v *Meugens* [1986] 1 FLR 125).

In *R* v *Blackpool Justices, ex parte Ardullis* (1981) *The Times,* 21 December, Sir John Arnold, President of the Family Division, sitting as an additional Judge of the Queen's Bench Division, said that it was open to the court to quash a decision of the justices to remit arrears of maintenance. In *R* v *Dover Magistrates' Court, ex parte Kidner* [1983] 1 All ER 475, an order for *certiorari* was granted and the decision to remit the arrears was quashed on the court's failure to comply with r 44 of the Magistrates' Court Rules 1981.

6. Power to search

The court can direct that the defendant be searched and may apply any money found in his possession in satisfaction of the arrears, unless the defendant can satisfy the court that the money does not belong to him or that the loss of it would be more injurious to his family than would be his detention (MCA 1980, s 80).

7. Arrears arising since complaint made

Fresh arrears which have become due since the complaint was made should be dealt with by the same court. An application to amend the complaint must be made, or a new complaint made and the old one withdrawn.

8. Notice of decision

The court must give notice in writing to the complainant of its decision on a complaint for the enforcement of a maintenance order, unless the complainant is present or is the justices' clerk (r 61 of the Magistrates' Court Rules 1981). No form of notice is prescribed by the rules.

9. Costs

The court has a discretion to order such costs as it thinks just and reasonable and, whatever adjudication it makes, the court can order either side to pay the whole or part of the other side's costs (MCA 1980, ss 64(1)(4)). Costs ordered against the defendant can be enforced with the maintenance arrears.

Appeal

1. Appeal by way of case stated

No appeal to the Crown Court is provided for, but appeal, by way of case stated, lies to the Family Division of the High Court (MCA 1980, s 111; and RSC, Ord 56, r 5(2)(*a*)). However, in *Snape* v *Snape* (1983) 13 Fam Law 210) the Family Division felt able to consider the question of arrears on the substantive appeal. Yet in *Mills* v *Mills* [1982] 12 Fam Law 174 the Family Division, in very similar circumstances, declined to treat the justices' refusal to remit arrears as part of the appeal on quantum of maintenance. In *Allen* v *Allen* [1985] 1 All ER 93 Booth J was not so reticent. Her Ladyship held that the justices' refusal to remit the arrears was part of their refusal to vary the order itself. Both the orders were made upon an application to vary and therefore the right of appeal to the High Court by way of notice of motion extended to the refusal to remit the arrears. A contrary view, however, was taken by Sir John Arnold in *Fletcher* v *Fletcher* [1985] 2 All ER 260. He stated that the remission of arrears under an application to vary was an intrinsic part of the enforcement procedure from which appeal was by way of case stated only. This was followed in *Berry* v *Berry* [1986] 2 All ER 948 and appeared to settle the matter beyond doubt. However, in *S* v *S* (1992) *The Times*, 8 December it was said by Thorpe J that an appeal from the refusal of justices to remit arrears which had accrued under a child's periodical payments order under the Children Act 1989 was by notice of motion to a judge of the Family Division under section 94 of that Act. In E v C (Calculations of Child Maintenance) [1996] 1 FCR 612, Douglas Brown J, however, intimated that for non-Children Act cases, *Berry* v *Berry* is the correct decision to follow.

In *R* v *Horseferry Road Magistrates' Court, ex parte Bernstein*, 151 JP 56 the question arose whether a magistrate could refuse to state a case on the ground that his decision was not final, since before the order of commitment to prison could be issued, the court was required to review the matter under s 18 of the MOA 1958. Sir John Arnold held that although a magistrates' court had power to review a committal order, the decision, even though on suspended terms, was a final one and suitable for argument on a case stated.

2. Appeal by way of judicial review

Application may be made in appropriate cases for judicial review. In *R* v *Dover Magistrates' Court, ex parte Kidner* [1983] 1 All ER 475 Woolf J stated that when judicial review is sought in respect of a matrimonial or family order, the application should include a request that it be heard by a Family Division judge rather than by a Queen's Bench Division judge. Proceedings by way of judicial review in relation to enforcement proceedings are in no way different to those in relation to orders or convictions in general, and are governed by the Rules of the Supreme Court.

Maintenance orders made against members of Her Majesty's forces

1. Deductions from pay made by the service authorities

The usual method of enforcing an order for the maintenance of dependants made against a person who is, or becomes, a member of Her

Majesty's Forces is by means of deductions from his pay by the service authorities. This is in accordance with the provisions of section 150 of the Army and Air Force Acts 1955 and section 1 of the Naval Forces (Enforcement of Maintenance Liabilities) Act 1947. See also Home Office Circular 251/1970 and 12/1982. The sums, payment of which may be enforced by this means, are sums due in respect of:

1. the maintenance of his wife, or of any child of his or his wife or of any other child who has been treated by them both as a child of their family
2. any costs incurred in obtaining the order; or
3. any costs incurred in proceedings on appeal against or for the variation, revocation or revival of the order

Note that reference to child of the dependent or his wife means whether or not they had been married at the time, or at any time.

2. Alternative to deductions from pay

There are, however, signs that the service authorities are finding the compulsory deduction of pay, regardless of willingness to pay, time-consuming and expensive (see Home Office Circular 25/1986). Consequently, the Ministry of Defence changed the procedures for the deduction of maintenance payments in respect of army personnel from 1 September 1985. The individual is now encouraged to make his own arrangements to meet his obligations under the court order. Should the serviceman disregard the court order or default at any time, application may then be made to the service authorities for enforcement of the order under section 150 of the Army Act 1955 and the Minimum Rates of Pay (Army) Order 1982.

3. Collection of arrears

A change has also taken place concerning the collection of arrears. In the past, army regimental paymasters kept a record of all arrears accruing, and recovered these arrears in instalments once the serviceman was in a position to pay. Under the revised procedure arrears will not be recovered automatically; the authorities suggest that it will be necessary for the complainant to obtain a further court order which, if made as a lump sum, can be enforced against pay under section 151A of the Army Act 1955. Precisely what sort of further order can be obtained in the magistrates' court remains a mystery, for in law the maintenance order and the arrears are indivisible. Furthermore, section 151A of the Army Act 1955 caters for the enforcement of civil debt, the definition of which, in the magistrates' court, specifically excludes maintenance payments. It should be emphasised, however, that these changes affect army personnel only.

4. Transmission of order to service authorities

A court making an order which is to be enforced by the service authorities by means of deductions from pay is required to send a copy of the order to the appropriate service authority as follows: the precise address of the relevant authority does vary and it is suggested that contact should be made with the court making the order; or with the Ministry of Defence or Lord Chancellor's Department.

5. Enforcement after cessation of service

In the case of former army and air force personnel the full range of enforcement powers, including committal, is available whether the arrears accrued before, during or after his service (Naval Forces (Enforcement of Maintenance Liabilities) Act 1947, s 1(3)). However, as regards the Royal Navy and Royal Marines, no committal may be ordered in respect of arrears accrued during the service of any seaman or marine unless the court is satisfied that he is able or has, since he ceased to serve, been able to pay the arrears, and has failed to do so.

6. Distress

A member of the armed forces is not immune from the execution of a distress warrant for the enforcement of a maintenance order, save as to the arms, ammunition, equipment, instruments or clothing used by him for naval, military or air force purposes (Army and Air Force Acts 1955, s185; Naval Discipline Act 1957, s 102). In practice, however, it would be highly unlikely that any bailiff would be allowed access to Ministry of Defence property to execute the warrant in respect of the defendant's personal property.

7. Reserve and auxiliary forces

The protection afforded by the Reserve and Auxiliary Forces (Protection of Civil Interests) Act 1951 does not extend to arrears under a maintenance order.

8. Visiting forces

The enforcement of an order made against a member of a visiting armed force will very much depend on whether that person is still within the jurisdiction. If so, then his position is no different from that of any other civilian, save that the Home Office has asked to be informed before any warrant of commitment is issued (Home Office Circular 122/1954). It is assumed that the diplomatic channels will be used to try to produce an amicable settlement. If the person has left the jurisdiction, enforcement will be reciprocal, subject to such arrangements existing.

CHAPTER 9

Imprisonment for Non-payment of Maintenance

CHAPTER 9

Imprisonment for Non-Payment of Maintenance

1. Introduction

Imprisonment is a sanction both harsh and severe in its consequences to the defendant and expensive to the state. In its effect upon a man's character, his family and dependants, the interruption of his work and the possibility of not finding work upon his release, it is often out of all proportion to the default of which he has been guilty. It is therefore essential that it should never be imposed without careful consideration, and should only be resorted to if it is the only practicable way of enforcing compliance with the law or with obligations which in the public interest must be enforced. It is particularly important that the sanction should not be used mechanically or automatically. The law does not require justices to commit where it is clearly undesirable to do so; see (*Grocock* v *Grocock* [1920] 1 KB 1).

Restrictions on use of imprisonment

1. Inquiry into cause of default

A magistrates' court cannot impose imprisonment for a default to which a complaint relates unless it has inquired, in the defendant's presence, whether the default was caused by the defendant's wilful refusal or culpable neglect; and it must not impose imprisonment if it is of the opinion that the default was not so due (MCA 1980, s 93(6)). The onus of showing to the justices' satisfaction that the default was not due to wilful refusal or culpable neglect is placed on the defendant (*James* v *James* [1963] 2 All ER 465, per Sir Jocelyn Simon P). However, in the light of recent High Court decisions requiring magistrates to justify their decisions more and more in respect of the use of imprisonment for non-payment, it is doubtful whether *James* v *James* is still good law. For the avoidance of any doubt it is preferable that justices do not operate under a presumption of "guilt" on the defendant's part; but actively base their finding of wilful refusal or culpable neglect on tangible evidence placed before the court.

2. Presence of defendant a prerequisite

A magistrates' court cannot impose imprisonment in the defendant's absence (MCA 1980, s 93(6)(*a*)). His presence at any previous hearing would not suffice.

3. Necessity to consider attachment of earnings order

A magistrates' court cannot impose imprisonment in a case in which it has power to make an attachment of earnings order unless it is of the opinion that such an order would be inappropriate. Quite clearly, where the circumstances of the case are such that the defendant would frustrate the order of the court by changing his employment frequently, an attachment of earnings order would not be appropriate (MCA 1980, s 93(6)(*b*)(i)).

4. Necessity to consider ordering payments by any method falling within MCA 1980, s 59(6)

Imprisonment in respect of default is further precluded (in a case where the court has power to do so) if it is of the opinion that it is appropriate to order that payments be made by any method of payment falling within section 59(6) of the MCA 1980. Section 59 provides a mandatory requirement on magistrates' courts to specify the method of payment in respect of maintenance orders requiring periodical payments. The court has the power to order that maintenance payments be made by one of four methods – direct to creditor, to the court, by standing order or by attachment of earnings order. Interestingly, the same powers are available to the High Court or county court, but their exercise is made discretionary so as not to affect any common law powers of the higher courts. Nevertheless, once a High Court or county court order is registered in the magistrates' court under the Maintenance Orders Act 1958, the mandatory requirement to consider ordering payments by the methods provided for in section 59(6) applies before imprisonment can be used.

5. Interest only debt

Imprisonment can not be imposed where the sum to which the default relates comprises only interest which the defendant has been ordered to pay by virtue of section 94A(1) of the MCA 1980. Regulations under this section have not yet been introduced (MCA 1980, s 93(6)(*b*)(*c*)).

Restrictions on detention of young persons aged 18 to 20 for default

It is not possible to commit a person aged under 18 to any form of custody for default (CJA 1982, s 9). This was confirmed by the Court of Appeal in *R* v *Basid* (1995) *The Times,* 19 October when dealing with a 17-year-old in respect of a confiscation order which was enforceable as a fine.

Where a court would, but for the general restriction on custodial sentences in relation to persons aged 18 to 20 have power to:

1. commit a young person to prison for default in payment of any sum of money, or
2. make a postponed committal order in the event of such default,

then the court may commit that young person to be detained, or may fix a term of detention in the event of default.

Any person dealt with in this way will be detained in one of the following places:

- a remand centre
- a young offenders institution
- in any place in which a person aged 21 or over could be kept for default in payment of a sum of money as the Secretary of State may from time to time direct (CJA 1982, s 12(10)).

The power to detain is subject to the proviso that the court must be of the opinion that no other method of dealing with the offender is appropriate (CJA 1982, s 1(5)). The reasons for reaching this opinion must be stated in open court and specified in the warrant and court register (CJA 1982, s 1(5A)).

In forming any opinion the court must take into account all the circumstances of the default (including any aggravating or mitigating factors) as are available to it; and may (discretionally) take into account any information about that person which is before it (CJA 1982, s 1(5)).

The term of imprisonment

The period for which a defendant may be committed to prison under a warrant of commitment must not exceed six weeks (MCA 1980, s 93(7)). The period contained in Schedule 4 of the MCA 1980 applies, as does the minimum period of seven days. For example, maintenance arrears under £1000 would not carry imprisonment in excess of 28 days, and arrears exceeding £1000 would be limited to a maximum of 42 days (see Home Office Circular 31/1979). Form 18 in the Magistrates' Courts (Maintenance Orders Act 1958) Rules 1959 is the prescribed form of warrant (Form 19 is the appropriate form where issue has been postponed).

A warrant of commitment, once issued, does not discharge the defendant from liability to pay the amount for which he was committed, although he cannot be committed again in respect of that amount or any part of it (MCA 1980, s 93(8); MOA 1958, s 17). The one exception would be where the court cancelled the warrant of commitment on review before the expiry of the term and placed the defendant on a suspended warrant of commitment for the amount remaining due.

Despite the fact that a warrant of commitment does not discharge the defendant, in practice collecting officers mark these arrears as unenforceable. It is submitted, however, that nothing will prevent the court from making an attachment of earnings order in respect of the arrears for which imprisonment has been served, since the prohibition only forbids re-committal, and does not affect any other method of enforcement.

In the unlikely event that a person is made the subject of two postponed committals to prison for non-payment of two separate maintenance orders, it is possible to order that the terms of imprisonment run consecutively up to a maximum period of 12 weeks. However, this may be done only when the terms are originally fixed, not on review under section 18 of the MOA 1958, since at that stage the court is not "imposing imprisonment" but simply issuing a warrant of imprisonment already imposed (note that "imposing imprisonment" includes fixing a term of imprisonment for failure to pay any sum of money).

Effect of committal on arrears

Unless the court directs otherwise (and very few will) no arrears will accrue while the defendant is in custody (MCA 1980, s 94). After release, the defendant may appropriate payments made to any new debt arising. In practice, however, few defendants take advantage of this and payments are appropriated against the earliest debt, ie the unenforceable debt for which imprisonment has already been served. Therefore, as the unenforceable arrears are discharged, further arrears accrue which are enforceable by imprisonment. A direction that arrears will accrue while he is in custody may properly be made where the defendant is deliberately avoiding the order (*Starkey* v *Starkey* [1954] 1 All ER 1036).

Postponing a warrant of commitment

Where a magistrates' court has power to issue a commitment warrant, it may, if it thinks fit to do so, fix a term of imprisonment and postpone the issue of the warrant until such time and on such conditions, if any, as it thinks just (MCA 1980, s 77(2)).

In practice a term of imprisonment will be suspended in this way either upon payment of a single periodical amount (sufficient to cover current dues and something towards the arrears); or, preferably, on payment of the current order and a further amount towards the arrears. It is inappropriate for a committal order to be suspended for payment only of an additional amount in relation to the arrears (*Fowler* v *Fowler* [1981] 2 FLR 141).

Failure to fulfil any conditions attached to the postponement may result in the warrant being issued after review, but arrears that have accrued since the original grant of the warrant cannot be added on; and further proceedings will be necessary to secure committal in respect of those new arrears (*R* v *Governor of Bedford Prison, ex parte Ames* [1953] 1 All ER 1002).

If the issue of the commitment warrant is postponed on condition that the defendant pay the order together with further payments to cover arrears to which the order does not apply, all amounts paid thereafter should first be appropriated to the arrears for which the committal order was made. This does not depend on the law relating to appropriation of payments, but solely on the statutory provisions relating to the power to commit, and the husband's right to avoid committal by paying the arrears (*R* v *Miskin Lower Justices, ex parte Young* [1953] 1 All ER 495; *Johnson* v *Johnson* [1946] 1 All ER 573). In this way the committal order remains throughout the sanction for the non-payment of the original debt only (ie the specific sum mentioned in the complaint and proved to the justices to be in arrears).

Finally, there is nothing to prevent justices imposing any other conditions they think just, subject of course to their being reasonable and relevant.

Power to review committals

1. Application not to have commitment warrant issued

Where a commitment warrant under section 77(2) of the MCA 1988 or section 18(3) and (5) of the MOA 1958 has been postponed, it must not subsequently be issued without further consideration (MOA 1958, s 18(1)). The clerk to the justices is required to give notice to the person liable to make payments under the order that if he considers there are grounds for not issuing the warrant, he may apply to the court in the prescribed manner, requesting that the warrant should not be issued and stating his grounds.

When dealing with orders not payable through his court, it is incumbent on the clerk to be extremely vigilant before acting on any notice of arrears supplied to him by the person entitled to receive payments.

Rule 22(1) of the Magistrates' Courts (Maintenance Orders Act 1958) Rules 1959 (the 1959 Rules) prescribes the form of notice to be used by the clerk, as well as providing for a prescribed form of application which is to be attached to the notice. Such notice is deemed to be given to the defendant if it is sent by registered post or recorded delivery to his last known address (MOA 1958, s 18(8)); notice is still deemed to have been given even if it is returned undelivered, or the defendant is known to have left that address (Re Follick, ex parte Trustee (1907) 97 LT 645). Forms 15 and 16 in the Schedule to the 1959 Rules are the prescribed forms of notice and application.

If, within eight days beginning with the day on which the clerk sends the notice to the defendant, the court has not received an application, then any justice of the peace acting for the same petty sessions area may issue the warrant of commitment (1959 Rules, r 22(3)). This seems to indicate that the justice has a discretion in the matter, but it is hard to envisage many circumstances where the exercise of a discretion not to issue the warrant would be proper, and one would normally expect the warrant to be issued fairly promptly.

If, however, an application is received within the eight days, then any justice, as above, may, after considering its contents:

1. if of the opinion that the application should be further considered, refer it to the court; or
2. if not of that opinion, issue the warrant forthwith.

Once again the justice involved has a limited discretion in the matter, although it has been said that he should always refer the matter to the court if there is a prima facie change in the defendant's circumstances (*Wood* v *Warley Justices* [1974] 4 Fam Law 130). Communications to a defendant at this stage, which could be interpreted as a modification of the notice given by the court of its intention to issue a warrant, should be sent by recorded delivery (*Slater* v *Calder Justices* [1984] 5 FLR 719). For example, if having served a notice, the defendant is subsequently informed that the warrant will not be issued, a fresh notice must be served before the commitment warrant can at a later date be issued.

If the application is to be referred to the court then section 18(2) of the MOA 1958 provides for notice to be given to the defendant, and to the person in whose favour the maintenance order was made, of the time and place appointed for consideration of the application. The non-attendance of either party does not preclude the court proceeding with the consideration of the application in their absence (MOA 1958, s 18(7)). No form of notice is prescribed by the rules.

2. Powers available to court on review

The following powers are available to the court on review:

1. remission of the arrears in whole or in part (MOA 1958, s 18(3)(6)); or
2. issue of the warrant (MOA 1958, s 18(3)(*a*)); or
3. further postponement of the warrant until such time and on such conditions, if any, as the court thinks just (MOA 1958, s 18(3)(*b*)); or
4. if in consequence of any change of the defendant's circumstances the court considers it appropriate to do so, an order that the warrant shall not be issued in any event (MOA 1958, s18(3)(*c*)).

Remission On considering an application referred to it by a single justice, a court may remit the whole or any part of the sum due under the order, in which case, either the order of commitment is discharged or the period of detention is reduced proportionately. Compliance, however, with Magistrates' Court Rules 1981 (notification to the person in whose favour the order is made etc) is not necessary since rule 44 relates solely to the power of remission contained in section 95 of the MCA 1980 which applies before commitment. The power to remit after commitment is contained in the MOA 1958 and no requirement similar to rule 44 exists other than by way of natural justice. In any event the person in whose favour the order was made is required to be given notice of the time and place of the hearing, and could attend to make representations.

Issue of the warrant Even after hearing the defendant's application, the court may order the commitment warrant to be issued forthwith. However, a substantial delay between the court giving notice of its intention to issue the warrant, and its actual issue could result in the need for a fresh notice of intention to be served (*Slater* v *Calder Justices* [1984] 5 FLR 719). Form 19 in the 1959 Rules is the prescribed form of warrant.

Further postponement of the warrant Clearly the court has wide powers to further postpone the issue of the commitment warrant on such terms as it thinks just. However, if this course is followed the warrant cannot be issued without the process being commenced again. A further problem can arise if the court decides to adjourn the proceedings. Has it in fact postponed the issue of the warrant until another time (in which case the process must be started again), or are the same proceedings being continued? While a court has an unfettered discretion to adjourn any proceedings, it is submitted that in this situation the court must adjourn only in proper circumstances, and in so doing clearly explain its intentions to the parties and record them in writing.

Order that the warrant shall not be issued in any event This is only exercisable if there is a change in the defendant's circumstances and only if the court considers it appropriate to do so. This precludes the court from going behind the original commitment decision.

Power to review where defendant already committed

1. Application by defendant already committed

Any defendant who is already imprisoned or detained under a warrant issued for the enforcement of a maintenance order may make an application to the court, requesting that the warrant be cancelled and stating the grounds of his application (MOA 1958, s 18(4)). Such an application cannot be made where the defendant is detained for some other reason. Form 17 MC in the 1959 Rules is the prescribed form of application.

On the receipt of any such application, a Justice of the Peace may:

1. refer it to the court if he is of the opinion that it should be further considered; or
2. if he is not of that opinion, refuse the application, in which case the defendant remains in custody and serves the remainder of the commitment.

A statement from solicitors on the defendant's behalf can be accepted as the disclosure of matters requiring further consideration (*Slater* v *Calder Justices* (1984)).

If the matter is referred to the court, the clerk must give notice to the defendant, the person entitled to receive payments and the person in charge of the prison or other place in which the defendant is detained of the time and place appointed for consideration of the application. The absence of any party to whom notice is required to be given does not preclude the court from proceeding with the consideration of the application. If the court is minded to remit the arrears in whole or part, additional compliance with rule 44 of the Magistrates' Court Rules 1981 is not strictly necessary (MOA 1958, s 18(7)). No form of notice is prescribed by the rules.

2. Powers available to the court on review

The following powers are available to the court on review:

1. remission of the arrears in whole or in part (MOA 1958, s 18(5)(6)); or
2. refusal of the application (MOA 1958, s18(5)(*a*)); or
3. where the court is satisfied that the defendant is unable to pay or to make any payment or further payment towards the sum outstanding, and it is of the opinion that in all circumstances the defendant ought not to continue to be detained under warrant, an order that the warrant shall cease to have effect when the person in charge of the prison (or other place) is informed of the making of the order (MOA 1958, s 18(5)(*b*)).

If the court does order that the warrant shall cease to have effect, it may, if it thinks fit:

1. fix a term of imprisonment in respect of the arrears remaining to be paid. The term must not exceed so much of the term of the previous warrant as remains to be served after taking account of any reduction occasioned by any of the arrears being remitted (MOA 1958, s 18 (5)(*b*)(i)); and
2. postpone the issue of a for the commitment warrant of the defendant for that term until such time and on such conditions, if any, as the court thinks just (MOA 1958, s 18(5)(*b*)(ii)).

As with an application made before committal, further postponements of the warrants will result in the whole review procedure having to be followed again before issue. It is submitted that here also the court must not go behind the decision which resulted in the original order of commitment, but must confine itself to circumstances arising or becoming known since the original commitment.

3. Notification to prison authorities and notice generally
Where the court cancels the commitment warrant, or remits the whole or any part of the sum for which the warrant was issued, then the clerk must forthwith give written notice of the decision to the person in charge of the institution in which the defendant is detained (1959 Rules, r 22(6)). No form of notice is prescribed.

Notice must be given to the person (if not present) in whose favour the maintenance order in question was made of any decision of the court pursuant to an application under section 18(1) or (4) of the MOA 1958 (1959 Rules, r 22(5)).

Notice must always be given to the defendant if he was not present, (except where an application under section 18(1) is dismissed since there is obviously little point in giving someone advance warning of their imminent arrest). No form of notice is prescribed.

Payment after imprisonment imposed

On payment of the full debt together with costs (if any), the commitment will cease to have effect, and the defendant will be released unless he is in custody for some other cause (MCA 1980, s 79(1)).

Where payment is made of only part of the sum due, this will have the effect of reducing the period of detention proportionately (MCA 1980, s 79(2)). The persons authorised to receive part-payment after imprisonment has been imposed are prescribed by rule 55 of the Magistrates' Court Rules 1981.

CHAPTER 10

Registration and Enforcement of Certain Maintenance Orders

CHAPTER 10

Registration and Enforcement of Certain Maintenance Orders

Introduction

"Maintenance order" in this context means any order specified in Schedule 8 to the Administration of Justice Act 1970 (MOA 1958, s 1(1A)). For the avoidance of any doubt the term also includes an order registered in a court in England and Wales under:

- Part II of the Maintenance Orders Act 1950
- The Maintenance Orders (Facilities for Enforcement) Act 1920
- Part I of the Maintenance Orders (Reciprocal Enforcement) Act 1972, or
- Part I of the Civil Jurisdiction and Judgments Act 1982.

In each case the order is deemed to be a maintenance order made by the court in which it is registered.

A High Court or county court order may be registered in a magistratesí court. A magistrates' court order may be registered in the High Court.

Neither a High Court order nor a magistrates' court order may be registered in a county court. However, a magistrates' court order registered in the High Court may still be enforced in the county court.

Whilst registered in the appropriate court, a maintenance order can be enforced in exactly the same manner as any order made by the court in which the order is registered. For example, an order registered in a magistrates' court under Part I of the Maintenance Orders Act 1958 is enforceable as a magistrates' court maintenance order (MOA 1958, s 3(2)).

Registration of High Court or county court order in magistrates' court

1. Application

Application for registration is to the court which made the order. That court has a discretion whether or not to allow registration (MOA 1958, s 2(1)). A certified copy of the maintenance order and two copies of the application in Form M33 must be lodged with the proper officer (Family Proceedings Rules 1991, r 7.23).

Practice Direction [1980] 1 All ER 1007, issued by the President of the Family Division, directed that applications for leave to register orders for nominal amounts in favour of spouses only should not be allowed, and, except in special circumstances, leave to register orders for maintenance pending suit and interim orders should not be granted.

Once the application to register is granted proceedings for the enforcement of the order before either registration or the expiration of the prescribed period (14 days in the High Court) (whichever occurs first) are prohibited (MOA 1958, s 2(2)). The original court must, within the prescribed period, send a certified copy of the order, accompanied by a copy of the application for registration, to the justices' clerk of the court in whose area "the defendant appears to be" (Family Proceedings Rules 1991, r 7.23(3)). The defendant need not "reside" in the area; he need only appear to be there. Consequently, there seems to be no basis on which a court can refuse to accept registration if the address given is within the jurisdiction.

If, however, at the end of the prescribed period the original court has not been satisfied by the applicant that proceedings for enforcement have not been begun, the grant of the application to register becomes void.

On receiving a certified copy of the order the magistrates' court clerk registers the order by means of a memorandum entered and signed by him in the court register (1959 Rules, r 4). The clerk must send a notice to the High Court or county court confirming that the order has been so registered. Notice must also be given to the defendant that payments have become payable to the magistrates' court clerk (this need not necessarily be the court of registration) (1959 Rules, r5 and Schedule, Form 8).

Alternatively, where a High Court or county court order is registered under the 1958 Act in a magistrates' court and a means of payment order (within the meaning of s 1(7) of the Maintenance Enforcement Act 1991) exists specifying the method of payment, then it shall continue to have effect after registration. However, this may in turn be varied or revoked by the magistrates' court in exercising its powers conferred by sections 4(2A), (5A) or (5B) of the MOA 1958.

2. Enforcement of orders registered in the magistrates' court

A registered order is enforceable as a magistrates' court maintenance order in every respect as if it had been made in the court in which it is registered and as if that court had jurisdiction to make it (MOA 1958, s 3(1)(2)(4)). While it is registered no other proceedings for the enforcement of the order are possible. In *Smith* v *Smith* [1976] 6 Fam Law 245) it was said that the magistrates' court should proceed to enforce an order even when an appeal is contemplated, unless the payer applies for and obtains a stay from the High Court or county court. Any person under an obligation to make payments under an order registered in a magistrates' court must give notice of any change of address to the clerk. Failure to do so, without reasonable excuse, renders that person liable to a fine not exceeding Level 2.

3. Discharge of order during or before registration

If the order remains or becomes registered after the discharge of the order the only enforcement proceedings possible are in relation to arrears which were due at the time of discharge (MOA 1958, s 3(3)).

4. Cancellation of registration

If the person entitled to receive payments under a registered order wishes the registration to be cancelled, notice may be given to the court of registration (MOA 1958, s 5(1)). If that person is the clerk to the justices, notice cannot be given (presumably to himself in most cases) unless he has been requested in writing to do so by the person entitled to receive payments through him (MOA 1958, s 20(1)). The clerk must comply with the request unless it appears to him to be unreasonable in the circumstances to do so.

In any proceedings taken by the clerk, it is the person who requested him to do so who is liable for costs, and not the clerk.

On giving of notice to cancel registration, no proceedings for the enforcement of the registered order are to be begun before the cancellation of the registration (MOA 1958, s 5(4)(*a*)). Furthermore no writ, warrant or other process for the enforcement of the order is to be issued in consequence of any such proceedings having been begun before the giving of the notice. Except where the defendant has already been detained in pursuance of the warrant, any commitment warrant already issued for the enforcement of the order ceases to have effect once the person in possession of the warrant has been informed that notice has been given (MOA 1958, s 5(4)(*b*)).

Registration of the order must be cancelled if the court of registration is satisfied by certificate that no process for the enforcement of the registered order, issued before giving of the notice, remains in force, and that no proceedings for variation are pending in a magistrates' court (MOA 1958, s 5(4)(*c*)). Form 3 in the 1959 Rules is the prescribed certificate that no enforcement or variation proceedings are pending.

On cancellation of registration the clerk must give notice to the High Court or county court, as the case may be, stating whether cancellation was in consequence of notice given by the person entitled to receive payments (1959 Rules, r 7(3)(5)). Proper notice is effected by a certified copy of the order being sent to the appropriate court stating, in the case of a High Court maintenance order, the title and cause number (if any); and in the case of a county court maintenance order, the plaint or application number (1959 Rules, r5(5)). Notice must also be given to the defendant and to the clerk of any court through which payments are being made. Form 10 in the Schedule to the 1959 Rules is the prescribed form of notice to the defendant.

The clerk has a duty to record particulars of the cancellation in the court register and to notify any person who is in possession of a commitment warrant which has not been executed (1959 Rules, r 8).

5. Effect of cancellation on payments

On the cancellation of the registration of a High Court or county court order:

1. any order which requires payments to be made by any method falling within section 59(6) of the Magistrates' Courts Act 1980 or section 1(5) of the Maintenance Enforcement Act 1991 (standing orders, etc) will continue to have effect *(other than payments to the magistrates' court clerk)*;
2. any order made which requires payment under the order in question to be made to the magistrates' court clerk (whether or not by any method of payment falling within section 59(6) of the Magistrates' Courts Act 1980) will cease to have effect.

In the latter case, until the defendant receives the proper notice of cancellation he shall be deemed to comply with the High Court or county court order if he continues to make payment in accordance with the order in force immediately prior to cancellation (MOA 1958, s 5(5)).

Registration of magistrates' court order in the High Court

1. Application

A person entitled to receive payments under a magistrates' court order who considers that it could be more effectively enforced if it were registered in the High Court may apply for registration to the court which made the order (MOA 1958, s 2(3)). The person "entitled to receive payments" could include a justices' clerk, but he may not apply for registration unless he is requested to do so in writing by the person entitled to recover payments through him (MOA 1958, s 20(1)). On receiving such a request the clerk must comply with it unless it appears to him unreasonable in the circumstances to do so.

The application need not be in writing or on oath (1959 Rules, r 1), although it may be prudent for it to be so. The court may then, *if it thinks fit,* grant the application. While it used to be a requirement that arrears of at least four weekly payments (or at least two payments in the case of orders not payable weekly) existed before the court allowed registration, this is no longer the case.

It is possible to apply for the separate registration of a lump sum order where the person entitled to receive the lump sum considers that that sum could be more effectively enforced if registered in the High Court (MOA 1958, s 2(3A)). Once again the court may, *if it thinks fit,* grant the application and, if it does, the lump sum is to be treated for the purpose of registration as if it were a separate order. Note, however, that this is a specific provision to lump sums only; it does not provide a general ability to dissect orders and have different parts in different courts. Even if orders were considered in law to be divisible (which is doubtful) it would lead to much confusion in terms of paying, accounting and enforcing.

Once an application for registration in the High Court is granted, no proceedings for the enforcement of the order are to be begun *before* the registration takes place, and no warrant or other process for the enforcement of the order is to be issued in consequence of any proceedings begun before the start of the application (MOA 1958, s 2(4)(*a*)).

Any commitment warrant issued for the enforcement of the order ceases to have effect when the person in possession of the warrant is informed of the grant of the application, unless the defendant has already been detained in pursuance of the warrant (MOA 1958, s2(4)(*b*)).

The clerk must certify to the court that no process for enforcement remains in force before a certified copy of the order is sent to the proper officer of the High Court (MOA 1958, s2(4)(*c*)). Form 2 in the Schedule to the 1959 Rules is the prescribed form of certificate that no process remains in force, and Form 7 is the prescribed certificate that the order is a true copy.

On receipt of the certified copy the appropriate officer must cause the order to be registered in the High Court by making an entry in the register or cause book and giving notice to the justices' clerk that the order has been duly registered. The details of the registration by the clerk must be entered in his register (1959 Rules, r 8).

Notice must also be given to the person liable to make payments that payment under the magistrates' courts order (or an order made by a sheriff court in Scotland, or a court of summary jurisdiction in Northern Ireland) and registered in a magistrates' court under Part II of the MOA 1950 has, on its registration in the High Court, ceased to be payable to the magistrates' court clerk (1959 Rules, r 5(2)). Where payments have been payable through a clerk other than the clerk of the administering court, a copy of the notice must be sent to that clerk. Form 9 in the Schedule to the 1959 Rules is the prescribed form of notice that payments have ceased to be payable through the magistrates' court clerk.

Where a magistrates' court order is registered in the High Court and payments are required to be made (otherwise than to the magistrates' court clerk) by any method falling within section 59(6) of the MCA 1980 (standing order, etc) then any order requiring payment by that method will continue to have effect after registration (MOA 1958, s 2(6)).

2. Enforcement of orders registered in High Court

A magistrates' court order is enforceable in the High Court in all respects as if it had been made by the High Court and as if that court had the jurisdiction to make it (MOA 1958, s 3(1)). While registered no other proceedings can take place.

It will, of course, be extremely rare for a magistrates' court order to be registered in the High Court. However, the High Court does have superior, and in some cases, unusual, powers (see *Thaha* v *Thaha* [1987] 2 FLR 142) which in some circumstances might be more appropriate. An example of this is where there is a very large lump sum order to enforce, or where the order, though deemed for the purpose of section 2A of the MOA 1958 to have been made by a magistrates' court in England, was in fact made in another part of the UK or in a country or territory outside the UK and interest can be claimed on the sum outstanding. For most people, however, there will be no practical advantage in a High Court registration.

3. Cancellation

Cancellation is effected by the person entitled to receive payments (including the justices' clerk if requested to do so in writing) giving notice to the appropriate officer of the High Court (MOA 1958, s 5(1)(4)). This will be the prescribed officer to whom a certified copy of the order has been sent pursuant to s2(4)(*c*) of the MOA 1958. Once this has been done, no proceedings for the enforcement of the registered order can be commenced before the cancellation of the registration, and no writ, warrant or other process for enforcement can be issued in consequence of any proceedings begun before the giving of the notice.

The High Court, on being satisfied by affidavit that no process for enforcement remains in force, must then cancel the registration (Family Proceedings Rules 1991, r 7.29). It must give notice to the clerk of the court which made the order (and where applicable to the clerk of the magistrates' court in which the order was registered in accordance with s17(4) MOA 1950) stating, if such be the case, that cancellation was in consequence of a notice given by the person entitled to receive payments.

Registration of English orders in Scotland and Northern Ireland

1. Orders which can be registered for enforcement

Registration is the only method of enforcing a maintenance order made by a court in England when the defendant resides in either Scotland or Northern Ireland (Part II of the MOA 1950). Parliament conveniently enacted that for legal purposes any reference to "England" was to include Wales, and, for the avoidance of doubt, Berwick-on-Tweed. (Wales and Berwick Act 1746, s 3).

Any of the following orders made by a court in England may if registered be enforced under section 16 of the MOA 1950 in Scotland or Northern Ireland:

1. an order made under sections 15–17, 19–22, 30, 34 and 35 Matrimonial Causes Act 1965, sections 22, 23(1), (2) and (4), and section 27 of the Matrimonial Causes Act 1973 and section 14 or section 17 of the Matrimonial and Family Proceedings Act 1984;
2. an order made under Part I of the Domestic Proceedings and Magistrates' Courts Act 1978;
3. Schedule 1 to the Children Act 1989
4. an order made under paragraph 23 of Schedule 2 to the Children Act 1989, or section 43 of the National Assistance Act 1948;
5. an order made under section 18 of the Supplementary Benefits Act 1976;
6. an order made under section 106 of the Social Security Administration Act 1992.

2. Procedure

In the case of a maintenance order made by a court of summary jurisdiction in England, application must be made by or on behalf of the person entitled to payments to a justice acting for the same place as the court which made the order (MOA 1950, s 17; Maintenance Orders Act 1950 (Summary Jurisdiction) Rules 1950 (the 1950 Rules), r2(1)). Application may be made orally or in writing but unless the applicant appears in person a statutory declaration must be lodged by the applicant, with the clerk, containing the following:

1. the address of the person liable to make payments under the order;
2. the reason why it is convenient that the order should be enforced in Scotland or Northern Ireland;
3. the amount of any arrears (only in cases where payments are not made through the clerk);
4. a declaration that the order is not already registered (1950 Rules, r 2(2)).

No form of application is prescribed by the rules.

If it appears to the justice dealing with the application that the person liable to make payments resides in Scotland or Northern Ireland, and that it is convenient for the order to be enforced there, then the clerk of the court is to send to the appropriate officer of the court in Scotland or Northern Ireland the following:

1. a certified copy of the order;
2. the certificate of arrears (see Form 3 in the 1950 Rules for the prescribed form) or statutory declaration (if any);
3. written notice of the address of the person liable to make payments (only if no statutory declaration has been lodged).

The appropriate officer will be, in Scotland, the sheriff clerk of the sheriff court which has jurisdiction in the area where the defendant appears to be; or, in Northern Ireland, the clerk of the court of summary jurisdiction having the same jurisdiction. Full details of courts in Scotland and Northern Ireland can be found in *Shaw's Directory of Courts in the United Kingdom,* and in cases of uncertainty the Lord Chancellor's Department will provide the appropriate address on request.

When registered, notice of the registration is to be given by the appropriate officer in Scotland or Northern Ireland to the clerk of the magistrates' court which made the order, who, in turn, must cause details to be entered in his own register (MOA 1950, s 17(4); 1950 Rules r 2(4)).

Note that while the defendant must *reside* in Scotland or Northern

Ireland for the purpose of a justice determining whether registration should take place, the clerk need only send the particulars to the court having jurisdiction where the defendant "appears" to be. It is clear that Parliament intended the defendant's presence in either Scotland or Northern Ireland to have some degree of permanence, but how much is a matter of debate. "Residence" obviously indicates an address (which is confirmed by the rules), and it is submitted that this would be sufficient in most cases. However, it may well be that only a "care of" address or even a "box number" address is known, and in these cases "residence" is a question of fact and degree (see *R* v *Edgehill* [1963] 1 All ER 181).

As to the requirement that it should be convenient that the order be enforced in Scotland or Northern Ireland, if the applicant satisfies the justice concerned that the defendant is "resident" there, it is difficult to envisage when it would not be convenient to enforce there, particularly as it is the only remedy available to the applicant.

Where payments are made through the justices' clerk he must, if requested to do so by the person entitled to payments, make an application for registration on that person's behalf, but that person still remains liable for costs (MOA 1950, s 17(6)).

The clerk is required to enter in the court register a memorandum of any proceedings taken in relation to an application for registration in Scotland or Northern Ireland, and on receipt of the notice of registration he must also cause particulars of that notice to be registered by means of a memorandum entered and signed by him in the register (MOA 1950, s 17(5); 1950 Rules r2(4)).

3. Re-registration of maintenance orders in Northern Ireland

Where a magistrates' court order has already been registered in a court of summary jurisdiction in Northern Ireland under Part II of the MOA 1950, an application may be made to the court which made the order ("the original court") for its re-registration in the Northern Ireland High Court (Civil Jurisdiction and Judgment Act 1982, s 36). The court of summary jurisdiction in Northern Ireland is then unable to enforce the order so long as it is registered in another court. Re-registration in this manner is of value only where interest is recoverable.

4. Enforcement of registered orders in Scotland and Northern Ireland

While registered, the order can be enforced in every respect by the court of registration as if that court had made the original order and had had jurisdiction to make it (MOA 1950, s 18(1)). Parties seeking registration in

Scotland should be made aware, however, that there are no collecting officers in Scotland and that it is not normal for the court itself to enforce the order. Parties are advised to instruct a lawyer in Scotland to act on their behalf.

5. Effect of registration

While an order is registered in either Scotland or Northern Ireland under Pt II of the MOA 1950 the following provisions apply (MOA 1950, s 19(1); 1950 Rules, r 13(2)):

1. the order cannot be registered for enforcement in any other court (MOA 1950, s 17(7));
2. no proceedings for enforcement can be taken by any court in England (MOA 1950, s 18(6));
3. any provision in the order requiring payments to be made through the justices' clerk is of no effect as long as the order remains registered. The clerk is under a duty to notify the defendant by registered post or recorded delivery at his last known address that the payments through him have ceased to be so payable;
4. whilst registered in a court of summary jurisdiction in Northern Ireland, an English or Welsh magistrates' court's order is enforceable under the Summary Jurisdiction (Separation and Maintenance) (Northern Ireland) Act 1945. This includes the power to specify the method of payment.

Form 2 in the Schedule to the 1950 Rules is the prescribed form. Until he is given the prescribed notice the defendant is deemed to comply with the maintenance order if he makes payments in accordance with that maintenance order (MOA 1950, s 19(4)).

6. Cancellation

An application for the cancellation of registration may be made at any time to the clerk or sheriff clerk of the court in which the order is registered, by or on behalf of the person entitled to payments (MOA 1950, s 24(1)(2)). It is advisable that the application be in writing (stating the date of registration), enclosing a copy of the order the registration of which it is sought to cancel. Upon receiving such an application the clerk must cancel the registration and send written notice of the cancellation to the clerk of the court which made the order. On receipt of such notice the clerk must cause particulars of the same to be registered in his court by means of a memorandum. No form of application or notice is prescribed by the rules for use in Scotland or Northern Ireland.

An application for the cancellation of the registration may also be made, either orally or in writing, by or on behalf of the person liable to make the payments, to a justice acting for the same place as the court which made the order (MOA 1950, s 24(2)). Unless the applicant attends in person he must lodge with the clerk a statutory declaration stating the facts upon which he relies in support of his application, namely that he has ceased to reside in Scotland or Northern Ireland as the case may be (1950 Rules, r 5(1)). No form of application is prescribed by the rules.

If it appears to the justice dealing with an application that the person liable to make payments under the order has ceased to reside in either Scotland or Northern Ireland, he must have the clerk send notice of this to the clerk of the court in which the order is registered, who will then cancel the registration of the maintenance order (1950 Rules, r 5(2)). Written notice of the cancellation must be sent to the clerk of the court which made the order and he must enter the particulars in the court register. Regardless of who the applicant was, notice of cancellation must be given to the person liable to make payments by the court cancelling the registration. Any provision in the original order requiring payments to be made to or through an officer of any court is revived. However, until he receives notice of the cancellation, he is deemed to comply with the maintenance order if he makes payments in accordance with any order which was in force immediately before the cancellation. No forms for use in Scotland or Northern Ireland are prescribed by the rules.

Registration in England of maintenance orders made by courts in Scotland or Northern Ireland

1. Orders which can be registered for enforcement

Part II of the MOA 1950 provides fully reciprocal arrangements between courts in England, Scotland and Northern Ireland for the enforcement of maintenance orders made in those countries. Hence, just as English orders can be registered in Scotland or Northern Ireland, so too can orders from either of those countries be registered in England.

The following orders from Scotland can be registered in England under section 16 of the MOA 1950:

1. a decree for payment of aliment granted by a court in Scotland including an order:
   - for payment of aliment of an annual or periodical allowance under section 2 of the Divorce (Scotland) Act 1938;
   - for the payment of a periodical allowance;

- for payment of a capital sum under section 26 of the Succession (Scotland) Act 1964 or section 5 of the Divorce (Scotland) Act 1976 or section 29 of the Matrimonial and Family Proceedings Act 1984;
- for financial provision in the form of a monetary penalty under section 8 of the Family Law (Scotland) Act 1985;

2. an order for the payment of weekly or periodical sums under section 3(2) or 5(4) of the Guardianship of Infants Act 1925;
3. an order for the payment of sums in respect of aliment under section 1(3) of the Illegitimate Children (Scotland) Act 1930;
4. a decree for payment of aliment under section 44 of the National Assistance Act 1948 or section 26 of the Children Act 1948;
5. an order under section 43 of the National Assistance Act 1948;
6. an order for the payment of weekly or other periodical sums under section 11(3) of the Guardianship Act 1973;
7. an order made on an application under section 18 or section 19(8) of the Supplementary Benefits Act 1976;
8. a contribution order under section 80, or a decree or an order made under section 81 of the Social Work (Scotland) Act 1968;
9. an order made on an application under section 106 of the Social Security Administration Act 1992

An order for alimony, maintenance or other payments made by a court in Northern Ireland may be registered in England under or by virtue of any of the following enactments:

1. section 17(2), section 19(2)–(7), section 20(2), 22 or section 28(1) of the Matrimonial Causes (Northern Ireland) Act 1939;
2. the Summary Jurisdiction (Separation and Maintenance) (Northern Ireland) Act 1945;
3. section one of the Illegitimate Children (Affiliation Orders) (Northern Ireland) Act 1924, section 159 of the Children and Young Persons (Northern Ireland) Act 1968 or Article 102 of the Health and Personal Social Services (Northern Ireland) Order 1972;
4. section 156 of the Children and Young Persons (Northern Ireland) Act 1968 or Article 101 of the Health and Personal Social Services (Northern Ireland) Order 1972;
5. any enactment of the Parliament of Northern Ireland containing provisions corresponding with section 22(1), 34 or 35 of the Matrimonial Causes Act 1965, section 22, 23(1), (2) or (4) or 27 of the Matrimonial Causes Act 1973, or section 12(2) of the Guardianship of Minors Act 1971;

6. Article 23 or 24 of the Supplementary Benefits (Northern Ireland) Order 1977;
7. the Domestic Proceedings (Northern Ireland) Order 1980;
8. any enactment applying in Northern Ireland and corresponding to section 106 of the Social Security Administration Act 1992;
9. Article 18 or 21 of the Matrimonial and Family Proceedings (Northern Ireland) Order 1989.

2. Procedure

Application for the registration of an order in England must be made by or on behalf of the person entitled to payments to the "appropriate authority". Where the maintenance order was made by a court of summary jurisdiction in Northern Ireland the appropriate authority is a resident magistrate acting for the petty sessions district of the court which made the order. In Scotland it is the prescribed officer of the court which made the order.

A statutory declaration or affidavit regarding the amount of the arrears must accompany the application and, in the case of payments made to or through an officer of the court (Northern Ireland only) a certificate, also signed by that officer, regarding the amount of any arrears due under the order (MOA 1950, s 20(1)).

If it appears to the appropriate authority that the person liable to make payments resides in England, and that it is convenient that the order should be enforceable there, the application must be granted and a certified copy of the order, together with the certificate, affidavit or statutory declaration, sent to the appropriate court in England (MOA 1950, s 17(2)). This will be the High Court if the order to be registered was made by a superior court, and in all other cases the magistrates' court acting for the place in England where the defendant appears to be.

On receipt of the order the clerk must register it by means of a memorandum entered and signed by him in the court register (MOA 1950 Rules, r 7). Notice has then to be sent to the court which made the order confirming that it had indeed been duly registered.

3. Effect of registration

Every maintenance order registered under Part II of the MOA 1950 in a magistrates' court in England is enforceable as a magistrates' court maintenance order in all respects as if it had been made by that court and as if that court had jurisdiction to make it (MOA 1950, s 18). It follows therefore that enforcement proceedings cannot be taken by any other court in England except on behalf of the court of registration. However, the order can be registered in the High Court in England under Part 1 MOA 1958 but may not then be enforced under Part II of the MOA 1950 to the extent that it is for the time being registered (MOA 1950, s 18(3A)).

While registered in England, the court of registration must, unless it is satisfied that it is undesirable to do so, order that all payments to be made under the maintenance order (including any arrears accrued before the date of registration) are to be paid through the court collecting officer, or the collecting officer of some other magistrates' court. Such an order may be varied or revoked by the court exercising its powers under section 18(2ZA). However, until the person liable to make payments under the order is given notice to this effect, he is deemed to comply with the maintenance order if he makes payment in accordance with last existing instructions. Form 1 is the prescribed form of notice to the defendant. (MOA 1950, s 19(2), (3) and (4)).

4. Cancellation

The procedure for the cancellation of a registration in England of an order made in Scotland or Northern Ireland is precisely the same as for the cancellation of the registration of an English order registered in Scotland or Northern Ireland.

5. English commitment warrants: execution in Scotland or Northern Ireland

Where a defendant moves to either Scotland or Northern Ireland after an English court has imposed a suspended period of imprisonment for the non-payment of maintenance, and that warrant falls to be issued, then the provisions of Part II of the MOA 1950 should not be required. This is because the Indictable Offences Act 1848 is applied to commitment warrants by section 126 of the MCA 1980. Therefore, provided the warrant is endorsed for execution in accordance with either section 12 or section 14 of the 1848 Act, the defendant should be arrested and brought back to England.

Furthermore section 136 of the Criminal Justice and Public Order Act 1994 (operative from 3 February 1995 as a consequence of Commencement Order No 3) applies not only to persons charged with "offences", but to "warrants of commitment" issued by any Justice of the Peace. Section 136 allows for a warrant issued in England, Wales or Northern Ireland to be executed in Scotland by any constable of any police force of the country of issue or of the country of execution as well as by any other person within the directions of the warrant (s 136(1)). Similarly, a warrant issued in Scotland or Northern Ireland can be executed in England and Wales (s 136(2)) and a warrant issued in England and Wales and Scotland can be executed in like manner in Northern Ireland (s 136(3)). Note, however that the provision is restricted to warrants of commitment only and does not apply to arrest warrants generally in respect of enforcement proceedings.

PART 5: ENFORCEMENT OF CHILD SUPPORT

CHAPTER 11

The Child Support Act 1991

CHAPTER 11

The Child Support Act 1991

Introduction

In April 1993, the Child Support Act 1991 came into effect. To say that this is a controversial piece of legislation would be an understatement. There are those who believe that the Act places the proper maintenance of children as the highest priority; and there are those who believe that the Act had less to do with putting "children first" (as the title of the Government's White Paper inferred) and more to do with reducing the cost of state benefit to single, divorced and separated parents. Regardless of where one stands on the political debate there is broad agreement that the legislation is complex and bureaucratic in its operation. It is interesting to note that the new Act requires several thousand civil servants based locally and regionally to operate it, whilst the magistrates' courts (who were previously charged with the task of collecting all maintenance) had only a few hundred staff in the whole of England and Wales. The difference in numbers was originally justified by reference to the expected improvement in collection rates which the new Act and the new Child Support Agency would achieve. Some three years later a number of pertinent questions are being asked over whether the new procedure is delivering value for money.

The Assessment

Applications fall to be made to the Child Support Agency (CSA) in two circumstances. The first is where the person with care of the child(ren) is not receiving state benefit (s 4). In effect this is a voluntary application but no right exists to make application to the courts any longer if the child fits within the definition of a "qualifying child". The second is where the person with care is receiving benefit (s 6). This section is more prescriptive and requires a person to authorise the CSA to recover child maintenance from the absent parent. In either case, the CSA will use the "maintenance formula" as prescribed by regulation to assess the level of maintenance due. The formula is standard to all cases and looks at the ability of both parents to provide the ideal level of maintenance support.

Various allowances and premiums are used to calculate the income available after basic needs have been met. The calculation is based is around a set of algebraic formulae contained in the Act itself; whilst the values of the various elements in the formula are to be found in secondary legislation. Once calculated, the assessment can be subject to a variety of reviews and appeals through to the Child Support Appeal Tribunal. Appeals on questions of law lie from the Child Support Commissioner to the Court of Appeal. Once the assessment has been made and all appeals and reviews have been exhausted, the collection and enforcement process must regard the assessment as being correct.

Collection

The collection of maintenance assessed under the 1991 Act is governed by section 29. In effect there are two alternatives:

1. where a person is receiving state benefit, the CSA will make the collection arrangements on its own initiative;
2. where the assessment has been made under section 4 (benefit not payable) either the person with care or the absent parent can ask the CSA to arrange collection; in such cases a fee is payable.

The collection of child maintenance by the CSA is governed by regulations made under section 29(2); and these are the Child Support (Collection and Enforcement) Regulations 1992 (SI No 1989) (the 1992 Regulations). The various methods of payment are very similar to those that can be ordered by the courts under the Maintenance Enforcement Act 1991. It may actually be that collection is being undertaken both by the CSA and the courts in respect of child and spouse maintenance respectively.

Enforcement

Enforcement is dealt with in sections 30–41 of the 1991 Act and in the 1992 Regulations. The powers available to the CSA are extensive and include a series of measures which require no recourse to the courts. Even when the courts become involved, their role is severely limited. The regulations bear a striking resemblance to the enforcement provisions created under the now repealed community charge legislation and the current council tax provisions. This is not coincidental since the community charge regulations were the model on which the CSA regulations were based.

The Various Enforcement Options

There are basically five enforcement options available to the CSA. The first, a deduction from earnings order, can be undertaken without reference to the courts. Thereafter some court involvement is required to a greater or lesser extent dependent on what is being sought. With the exception of garnishee and charging orders, all court remedies are available from the magistrates' court. The complete range of enforcement options are:

- deduction from earnings orders (DEO)
- liability orders
- distress
- garnishee and charging orders
- imprisonment

Deduction from earnings orders

Section 31 of the 1991 Act authorises the CSA to deduct payments direct from earnings. This can either be as a first stage in the enforcement process or when another payment method has been tried but failed. In most cases, though, it will be the first choice before court action is contemplated since in order to move to the next stage of obtaining a liability order, the CSA will have to show that it was inappropriate to make a DEO, or that such an order has been made but has proved ineffective.

In many respects the DEO is identical to the attachment of earnings order (AEO) made under the Attachment of Earnings Act 1971. However, the new name for the order was intended to differentiate it from the court-based order and to emphasise its administrative nature. The DEO is authorised by legislation and not by the courts provided certain criteria are met.

1. Earnings

In order to deduct payments direct from "earnings" it is important to understand what that term means. Failure to do so can result in appeal to a magistrates' court under section 32(5) of the Act. Procedure is governed by regulation 22 of the 1992 Regulations and provides that an appeal is by way of complaint within 28 days of notification of the order being made. There are only two grounds of appeal. The first is that the "earnings" in question are not earnings as defined by law; and secondly, that the DEO is defective. In the latter case the court is precluded from questioning any aspect of the assessment itself (s 31(6)) and in practical terms it is difficult to envisage many appeals on this ground. The definition of "earnings" is complex and could result in a number of challenges.

Regulation 8 of the 1992 Regulations defines "earnings" as sums payable to a person in any of the following cases:

1. by way of wages or salary (including any fees, bonus, commission, overtime pay or other emoluments payable in addition to wages or salary or payable under a contract of service);
2. by way of pension (including any annuity in respect of past services, whether or not rendered to the person paying the annuity, and including periodical payments by way of compensation for the loss, abolition or relinquishment or diminution in emoluments, of any office or employment);
3. by way of statutory sick pay.

The following are specifically excluded from the definition of "earnings":

- sums payable by any public department of the Government of Northern Ireland or of a territory outside the United Kingdom;
- pay or allowances payable to the liable person as a member of HM Forces;
- pension, allowances or benefit payable under any enactment relating to social security;
- pension or allowances payable in respect of disablement or disability;
- guaranteed minimum pension within the meaning of the Social Security Pensions Act 1975.

2. The normal deduction rate and protected earnings rate

As with attachment of earnings orders, a DEO must have both a normal deduction rate and a protected earnings rate. These are both defined by regulation as to what elements they may include.

Normal deduction rate (NDR) Regulation 8 of the 1992 Regulations defines the NDR as the amount the CSA specifies in respect of the various deductions set out below, namely:

- the amount due under the maintenance assessment in respect of the period to which the deduction relates;
- any arrears of child support maintenance;
- any periodical or secured periodical payment (including arrears)

which the Secretary of State has arranged to collect by virtue of the 1991 Act which authorises him to collect other forms of maintenance also due in respect of the period to which the deduction of child support maintenance relates;

- any interest on arrears payable under section 41(3) of the Act and relevant regulations.

Regulation 10(2) limits the scope of the CSA to specify the NDR further by preventing a person from specifying any amount in respect of arrears or interest if as a result the net income would fall below the protected earnings rate less a prescribed amount. (as defined by regulation).

Protected earnings rate (PER) As with attachment from earning, the PER is the minimum amount of money specified by legal formula which the debtor must be left with in his pay or salary. If there are insufficient money to deduct the NDR and leave the debtor with his protected rate, then a lesser amount (or possibly nothing) will have to be deducted on that occasion.

The calculation of the PER is to be found in regulation 11 and in broad terms is equal to the liable person's exempt rate as calculated at the date of the current assessment.

3. Employers

Not surprisingly, employers play a vital role in the DEO process. For their troubles they can deduct from the debtor up to £1 by way of an administrative charge for every deduction they operate under the order. This "charge" is outside the protected earnings framework and can be deducted even if the net result is that the debtor has £1 less in his pay than the PER would suggest.

The obligations placed on employers are not inconsiderable. Regulation 13 requires them to notify the employee of the amounts deducted (including fee) either on the payday when deduction is made or alternatively, on the following payday if that is not practicable. Regulation 14 prescribes the method by which the employer must pay the Secretary of State and at what intervals. Regulation 16(1)–(3) requires the employer to tell the CSA within ten days if he receives a DEO and the person named in it does not work for him; alternatively the employer has ten days to notify the CSA when a debtor leaves his employment. If an employer becomes aware that a debtor has joined his employment and a DEO exists but is not being operated by him, then he must notify the CSA within seven days. Breach of any of these requirements is a criminal offence and subject to a fine at level 2 (s 32(8)–(11)).

4. Duties on the debtor

Without precise details of employment, the DEO is inoperative. Consequently, the CSA has wide-ranging powers under regulation 15 to require a debtor to give a full range of information regarding his employment (if any). Similarly, the debtor must report any changes within seven days. Failure to comply with either of these provisions is a criminal offence punishable by a fine not exceeding level 2 on the standard scale (s 32(8)and (11)).

5. Miscellaneous

Regulations (18, 20 and 21) provide for the variation, discharge and lapse of DEOs, as well as for establishing priority between orders, by date, when more than one order is in existence. For these purposes an AEO is treated as the same as a DEO, except where the AEO is made in respect of a judgment debt or administrative order only; in such cases the DEO will always take priority (reg 24).

Liability orders

The concept of a "liability order" was first introduced by the Local Government Finance Act 1988. Despite the repeal of that infamous piece of legislation, the Child Support Act (Collection and Enforcement) Regulations 1992 were modelled, almost to the letter, on the Community Charge (Administration and Enforcement) Regulations 1989. This was unfortunate since the term "liability order" had became discredited; it was, therefore, not the most sophisticated piece of political marketing to use the same terminology in another equally controversial piece of legislation. Government officials were told this at the time but chose to ignore the advice, arguing that the concept of a "liability order" had been established by section 33 of the primary legislation (i.e. the 1991 Act) and it was therefore not capable of being changed.

1. Preconditions to obtain a liability order

The 1991 Act establishes a number of preconditions before application for a liability order can be made. These are:

1. the liable person must have failed to make one or more payments of child support maintenance; and
2. that it appears to the Secretary of State that it is inappropriate to make a DEO; or
3. that a DEO has been made, but has proved ineffective.

Like a civil debt order, the liability order simply confirms that the amounts of maintenance money claimed by the CSA are legally due and payable. Similarly, like a complaint for the enforcement of a maintenance order, the order deals only with the amount of money being claimed in respect of that particular court action. Further sums becoming due will be the subject of a new application.

2. Procedure

Procedure is governed by Part IV of the 1992 Regulations (as amended). Application is by way of complaint to a magistrates' court having jurisdiction where the liable person resides. The normal six-month time limits are extended to six years from the time payment was due. The liable person is entitled to at least seven days written notice of the CSA's intention to begin proceedings.

On determining whether to grant the liability order the court is precluded from questioning the original maintenance assessment under which payments fall to be made (s 33(4)). If satisfied that the payments in question have become payable and have not been paid, the Act requires the magistrates' court to make the order.

3. Defences

Given such little discretion it is difficult to envisage on what basis a successful challenge could made against the issue of such an order. Procedural irregularities such as insufficient notice or the complaint being made out of time are obvious enough. If it is asserted that payments have been made then this would be a simple matter of proof. Similarly, it may be possible to argue that the circumstances to make a DEO always existed and therefore the Secretary of State's assertion that it was "inappropriate" to make one may be questioned. Other than that the court is simply being asked to confirm the debt and there seems little opportunity to challenge liability at this stage. Nevertheless, the making of a liability order is not an insignificant event since a number of other enforcement options are now available to the CSA.

4. Distress

Distress will be the CSA's normal method of enforcing a debt once a liability order has been obtained. Statutory authority for distress can be found in section 35 of the 1991 Act, which states:

> *"where a liability order has been made against a person ('the liable person'), the Secretary of State may levy the appropriate amount by distress and sale of the liable person's goods."*

The "appropriate amount" is defined as meaning the arrears together with any charges connected with the use of distress. Schedule 2 to the 1992 Regulations contains the schedule of prescribed charges.

Regulation 30 of the 1992 Regulations contains the necessary procedures for levying distress. These are:

1. Distress can be levied in any part of England and Wales.
2. Any defect or want of form in the initial liability order will not render the distress unlawful on this ground alone.
3. Any person executing the distress warrant must carry the written authority of the Secretary of State and show this authority when requested to do so.
4. A copy of section 35 of the 1991 Act and any regulations made under that section must be handed to the liable person or left at the address where distress is levied. In addition the person levying distress must also provide a note setting out the amount to be levied and a copy of any agreement entered into by way of close or walking possession.
5. Full payment (including costs) will stop the distress action provided payment is made before goods are seized. After seizure and before sale, payment in full can be made but the return and collection of the goods are the responsibility of the discharged debtor.

5. Appeals against distress

Section 35(8) of the 1991 Act and regulation 31 of the 1992 Regulations appear to give an unlimited right of appeal against distress. These provisions state that any person aggrieved by the levy of, or an attempt to levy, distress has the right to appeal to a magistrates' court. In practice the appeals will be based on technical grounds such as a failure to observe procedure or the taking of exempt goods as defined by section 35. Theoretically, "any person" could include someone other than the debtor, where, for example, their goods have been distrained. If the court is satisfied that the distress was irregular the goods can be discharged and compensation awarded. Very few appeals have been brought to date and little or no guidance exists on what is "irregular" and what level of compensation should be awarded.

Costs can be appealed. A process exists for taxation by a district judge of the County Court. The process is *ex parte* and started by an originating application.

Charging and garnishee orders

These orders are outside the scope of magistrates' courts and are covered by normal county court procedures. A pre-requisite to any application is that distress has been attempted without success, or is considered inappropriate. The procedure is authorised by section 36 of the 1991 Act.

In *DSS* v *Butler* ((1995) *The Times,* 11 August), the Court of Appeal was asked to determine whether, as a matter of general principle, the High Court could assist a magistrates' court through the granting of injunctive relief (i.e. a Mareva order) for the preservation of assets. The Court of Appeal answered in the negative. The child support system was a creature of statute. The CSA's statutory right to seek a liability order was confined to the magistrates' court and was not one the High Court could enforce. Where the High Court had no substantive power, it could not exercise ancillary power. Furthermore, the 1991 Act was comprehensive. It not only deprived the High Court of any substantive powers, it gave it no ancillary, supportive or supervisory powers at all. Finally, the 1991 Act gave the CSA no right to anticipate the making of a liability order by magistrates.

Imprisonment

As always, the use of imprisonment is a harsh and final measure in the pursuit of debt. Where the CSA has attempted to enforce the maintenance due by distress (or by charging or garnishee orders) and failed, it can apply to a magistrates' court for the issue of a commitment warrant (CSA 1991, s 40). Curiously, if enforcement in the county court has been attempted, a fresh liability order is needed before imprisonment can be used.

The usual conditions regarding the use of imprisonment as outlined in other parts of this book apply , namely:

- the debtor must be present;
- attendance can be enforced by summons and/or a warrant (with or without bail);
- the court must be satisfied that non-payment was due either to wilful refusal or culpable neglect on the debtor's part;
- the commitment to prison can be immediate or suspended on terms;
- the commitment can include any costs incurred in the application;
- the maximum period of imprisonment or detention is six weeks

and Schedule 4 to the MCA 1980 applies up to that maxima;
- part-payment will reduce the period of commitment proportionally;
- new arrears must be the subject of a separate enforcement process starting with the consideration of a DEO and then an application for a new liability order.

The welfare of any child during the enforcement process

Section 2 of the 1991 Act provides a general duty on a child support officer to have regard to the welfare of any child likely to be affected by any decision he makes. This is a broad requirement and applies equally to the enforcement process as any other. "Child" in this context includes any child within the household of the absent parent. Consequently, decisions on whether to levy distress or seek a charging order should be made against the backcloth of this "welfare" criteria. In practical terms it seems that this provision has little practical effect since the interests of a child in the absent parent's home are counterbalanced by the interests of the child(ren) subject to the assessment. It may be, however, that specific needs such as disability may result in a particular form of enforcement being regarded as inappropriate in the light of section 2. Note that the CSA need only have regard to the child's welfare, not that the child's welfare is paramount.

PART 6: ATTACHMENT OF EARNINGS

CHAPTER 12

Attachment of Earnings

CHAPTER 12

Attachment of Earnings

Introduction

An attachment of earnings order (AEO) may be described as an instruction to an employer to make prescribed deductions from the debtor's earnings, the amounts deducted being sent by the employer to the clerk of the court specified in the order.

Section 1 of the Attachment of Earnings Act 1971 (AEA 1971) provides that a magistrates' court has power to make an AEO to secure the recovery of any sum adjudged to be paid by a conviction or treated (by any enactment relating to the collection and enforcement of fines, costs, compensation or forfeited recognisances) as so adjudged to be paid. This includes power to make such an order in respect of a legal aid contribution. Generally, a legal aid contribution order is treated as being enforceable as an affiliation order. For the purposes of attachment of earnings, however, this is not the case. All provisions relating to attachment of earnings to recover a sum adjudged to be paid by a conviction apply equally to a legal aid contribution order.

The court may also make an AEO to recover payments under a maintenance order enforceable in a magistrates' court.

Earnings

"Earnings" are defined under section 24 of the AEA 1971 as sums payable to a person by way of:

1. wages or salary (including any fees, bonus, commission, overtime, pay or other emoluments payable in addition to wages or salary payable under a contract of service);
2. pension (including an annuity for past services whether or not rendered to the person paying the annuity, and including periodical payments by way of compensation for the loss, abolition or diminution in emoluments, of any office or employment).
3. statutory sick pay

The following are not to be treated as earnings:

- sums payable by any department of the Northern Ireland government or other territory outside the United Kingdom;
- pay or allowances to the debtor as a member of HM Forces;
- pension or allowances or benefit payable under enactments relating to social security;
- pension or allowances payable in respect of disablement or disability (but not "ill health" pensions: see *Miles* v *Miles* [1979] 1 All ER 865);
- except in relation to a maintenance order, wages payable to a person as a seaman (but not a seaman of a fishing boat);
- guaranteed minimum pension within the meaning of the Pension Schemes Act 1993.

Application and procedure

Except in relation to a maintenance order, a court is not entitled to make an order of its own motion. It is a condition precedent to the making of an order that there should be a proper application. The court dealing with enforcement against an offender should not consider that it has power automatically to make an AEO when it becomes apparent that the offender is employed. There is a formal procedure which must be followed.

Application for an order may be made:

1. by the person to whom the payment under the relevant adjudication is required to be made (whether directly or through an officer of any court);
2. by the debtor;
3. in the case of a maintenance order under which payments are required to be made through the court clerk, by the clerk, but only where he is requested to do so by the person entitled to payments. The request must be in writing and, where such a request is made, the clerk must comply with the request unless it appears to him unreasonable in the circumstances to do so (AEA 1971, ss 3 and 18(1)(*a*)). Note that except in relation to maintenance orders, for an order to be made on the application of a person other than the debtor it must appear to the court that the debtor has failed to make one or more of the required payments under the relevant adjudication.

With regard to maintenance orders, the court can make an order either on application or by its own motion. A court may make an order of its own motion in proceedings brought to recover outstanding maintenance payments and the court may make an AEO instead of dealing with the case by the issue of a distress warrant or commitment warrant. Where the court makes an order of its own motion no formal application is required.

Where an application is required prior to making an AEO, the application is by way of complaint (AEA 1971, s 19(1)). No form of complaint is prescribed. The procedure to be adopted at the hearing is the same as for hearing complaints generally.

Where the application is made by the party to whom payment is required to be made, a summons should be issued to the debtor. Where application is made by the debtor, a summons should be issued to the person to whom payment is required to be made (whether directly or through an officer of any court) (AEA 1971, s 19(4)).

A complaint for an order may be heard notwithstanding that it was not made within six months of the date when the matter of complaint arose (AEA 1971, s 19(5)).

Power to obtain statement of earnings

Where a court has power to make an attachment of earnings order, it may under section 14(1) of the AEA 1971 order a debtor to give to the court within a specified period a statement signed by him of

1. the name and address of any person by whom earnings are paid to him;
2. specified particulars of his earnings and expected earnings and of his resources and needs; and
3. specified particulars for the purpose of enabling the debtor to be identified by an employer of his.

In addition, the court may order an employer to give to the court within a specified period a statement, signed by him or on his behalf, of specified particulars of the debtor's earnings and expected earnings.

The power to require such a statement may be exercised by a single justice or justices' clerk. It may be exercised before the hearing of the application or at any time after the AEO has been made (AEA 1971, s 14(2)). In the case of an application for the variation or discharge of an AEO, such a statement can be ordered before the hearing of the application.

A document purporting to be a statement given in compliance with such an order is, in the absence of proof to the contrary, deemed to be a statement so given and is evidence of the facts stated therein (AEA 1971, s 14(5)).

It is an offence not to comply with an order requiring a statement of earnings (AEA 1971, s 23(2)(*c*)). It is an offence to make a statement purportedly in compliance with such an order knowing that it is false in a material particular, or to make a statement recklessly which is false in a material particular (AEA 1971, s 23(2)(*f*)). In each case the maximum penalty on summary conviction is a fine not exceeding level 2 on the standard scale (AEA 1971, s 23(3)).

Power to make an order

1. Application otherwise than by debtor

Before the court can make an order on the application of a person other than a debtor, it must appear to the court that the debtor has failed to make one or more of the payments required by the relevant adjudication (AEA 1971, s 3(3)). Where payment by instalments has been allowed it may appear that although at some stage one or more payments were outstanding at the time they were required to be made, at the time of the hearing of the application for the AEO, payments have been "brought up to date". In such circumstances an order can still be made.

The debtor must be employed (AEA 1971, s 6(2)). For the purposes of attachment of earnings, the relation of employer and employee exists between two persons if one of them, as a principal and not as servant or agent, pays to the other earnings (for definition see p 142).

2. Application by debtor

It is not necessary for the debtor to show that there has been a failure to make any of the required payments. There is nothing to prevent an application being made by the debtor immediately following a conviction or the making of a maintenance order. Such a step having much to recommend it, the court could helpfully remind a debtor that it is open to him to make the application.

The order

1. Making the order

In making the order the court must decide the amount of the normal deduction rate (NDR) (AEA 1971, s 6(5)(a) and Sched 3, Pt I). This is the sum to be deducted from the debtor's earnings after allowance has been made for income tax, superannuation contributions, contributions under Part III of the Social Security Act 1983, and contributions under Part I of the Social Security Act 1975. It is for the court to decide the size of the normal deduction and the period over which it should be made. It must ensure that the sum to be deducted is reasonable in all the circumstances, the deduction being made with reference to a week, month or other period.

In the case of an order to secure maintenance payments, the normal deduction rate is to be determined after taking into account any right or liability of the debtor to deduct income tax when making the payment; it must not exceed the rate which appears to the court necessary to secure the payments required under the maintenance order plus payment within a reasonable period of any outstanding arrears.

The court must also set the protected earnings rate (PER) (AEA 1971, s 6(5)(*b*)). This may be described as the level below which earnings actually paid to a debtor should not be reduced. In determining the level of a PER, the court must take into account the debtor's resources and needs, including the needs of any person for whom he must, or reasonably may, provide. Should earnings on any pay-day be less than or equal to the PER, the normal deductions should not be made (AEA 1971, Sched 3, para 6(4)).

2. Contents of order

Section 6 of the AEA 1971 and rule 7 of the Magistrates' Courts (Attachment of Earnings) 1971 Rules, provide that the order must specify the NDR and the PER. In addition, the order must:

1. except where made to secure maintenance payments, specify the whole amount payable under the relevant adjudication (or so much of that amount as remains unpaid), including any relevant costs;
2. contain, so far as is known, the debtor's full name and address, his place of work, the nature of that work, and his works number if any;
3. specify the court to which deductions made by the employer should be transmitted. In making an order the court may direct that deductions be sent to the court which made the order or to the clerk of such other court as may be specified.

Copies of the order must be served upon both employer and debtor (1971 Rules, rr 6, 18 and 21). The employer should also be notified of the hours during which, and the place at which, payments are to be made and received. A copy of the order must also be given to the county court registrar for the district in which the debtor resides. The prescribed forms of order are Forms 1 and 2 contained in the Schedule to the 1971 Rules.

The Employer

The employer's liability to make the deductions does not begin until seven days have elapsed since the service of the order (AEA 1971, s 7(1)).

Where an employer is served with an order but he does not have the debtor in his employment, or the debtor subsequently ceases to be in his employment, the employer must within ten days from the date of the service or cesser of employment give notice of this to the court (AEA 1971, s 7(2)). In addition, where a debtor leaves one employer and joins another, that other must notify the court in writing that he is the debtor's new employer and must include in his notification a statement of the debtor's earnings and expected earnings (AEA 1971, s 15). An employer will only have to do this however, where he knows both that an order is in force and by what court it was made. The notification should be given within seven days of his becoming the debtor's employer or within seven days of his becoming aware of the order, whichever is later.

Any deductions made by an employer must be paid to the clerk of the court specified in the order (1971 Rules, r 18). Any payment sent by post will be sent at the employer's risk and expense.

The deduction required to be made by an employer on any payday is the specified normal deduction and is to be deducted under paragraph 4 of Schedule 3 to the AEA 1971 as follows:

1. where it is a debtor's first payday, by reference to the period for which he is being paid, beginning with the first day of his employment;
2. where it is not the first payday, then in the case where on the last payday payment was made in respect of a period falling wholly or partly after that payday, by reference to a period beginning with the first day after the period which payment has been made;
3. in any other case, by reference to a period beginning with the first day after the last payday and ending:
   (a) where payment is made in respect of a period falling wholly or partly after the payday, with the last day of that period (this will cover such items as holiday pay);
   (b) in any other case with the payday.

The PER is applied in the same way.

Before an employer is entitled to make the normal deduction, however, it must appear to him that attachable earnings on any payday exceed not only the PER for the relevant period, but also any sum by which on previous paydays attachable earnings fell short of the PER that has not been made good by subsequent earnings. Where such a situation exists then, once the shortfall in protected earnings has been made good by subsequent earnings, the normal deduction for the day in question, plus in so far as the excess allows, so much of the normal deduction that on a previous payday was not deducted, can be made.

The Debtor

While an order is in force the debtor must notify the court in writing of every occasion on which he leaves any employment, or becomes employed or re-employed, not later (in each case) than seven days from the date on which he did so (AEA 1971, s 15). In addition, the debtor must on any occasion when he becomes employed or re-employed include in his notification particulars of his earnings and expected earnings.

Failure to comply with order

1. The employer

An employer commits an offence if he fails to comply with an order, or fails to give the notices required above, or gives notice which he knows to be false in a material particular, or recklessly gives notice which is false in a material particular (AEA 1971, s 23(2)). In addition, an employer commits an offence if, in purported compliance with the requirement to give such notice, he makes a statement which he knows is false in a material particular or recklessly makes a statement which is false in a material particular.

An employer who commits such an offence renders himself liable on summary conviction to a fine not exceeding level 2 on the standard scale (AEA 1971, s 23(3)).

2. The debtor

A debtor commits an offence if he fails to give any notice required above, or gives a notice which he knows is false in a material particular, or recklessly gives a notice which is false in a material particular. He also commits an offence if, in purported compliance with any requirement above, he makes a statement which he knows is false in a material particular or recklessly makes such a statement.

A debtor who commits any such offence renders himself liable on summary conviction to a fine not exceeding level 2 on the standard scale (AEA 1971, s 23(3)).

Variation and discharge

1. General provisions

The court may make an order discharging or varying an AEO (AEA 1971, s 9). The application is by way of complaint. However it is not clear by whom such an application can be made; it is certainly not clear whether an employer is entitled to make the claim. It is submitted that the effect of section 19 of the AEA 1971 (procedure on applications) and section 51 of the MCA 1980, is to prohibit an employer from making such an application. Under Section 51 MCA 1980, a justice may, on the making of a complaint, issue a summons to a person against whom an order can be made. Section 19 provides that for this purpose, the power to make, vary or discharge an AEO on the application of the debtor shall be deemed to be a power to make an order against the person to whom payment under the relevant adjudication is required to be made (whether directly or through an officer of the court), and the power to discharge or vary an AEO on the application of any other person is deemed to be power to make an order against the debtor. Here it is submitted that the words "any other person" are limited to those persons against whom a summons could be issued and an order made on the application of the debtor. Hence an application for variation or discharge can be made by:

- the debtor, or
- the person entitled to the payments.

There are no specific provisions about the matters to be taken into account by the court in deciding whether to vary or discharge an order. The court should therefore take into consideration such matters that it considers reasonable when dealing with the application.

A copy of an order varying or discharging an AEO must be served on the employer, the debtor and the county court (1971 Rules, r 6).

No form of complaint, nor any form of order of discharge or variation is prescribed, although there is a prescribed form of temporary variation (Form 3 of Schedule to the 1971 Rules).

In the case of an order to secure maintenance payments, the clerk through whom payments are required to be made may not apply for the discharge or variation of the AEO unless requested in writing to do so by the person entitled to receive payments (AEA 1971, s 18(1)(*b*)). Where a request is made, the clerk must comply with the request unless it appears to him unreasonable in the circumstances to do so.

2. Temporary variation

It is open to a debtor, where there has been a material change in his resources and needs since the order was made or last varied, to apply for a temporary variation of the PER (AEA 1971, s 9(3); 1971 Rules, r 14). It must be in writing setting out details of the changed circumstances. The application may be made to a single justice or justices' clerk acting for the same petty sessions area as the court which made the order. No formal procedure is laid down. On being satisfied that there has been a material change in the debtor's circumstances, the justice or justices' clerk dealing with the application may by order vary the AEO, by increasing the PER for a period of not more than four weeks. A copy of the order for temporary variation must be served upon the employer. The order must be in the prescribed form.

3. Appropriate variation

In the case of an order made to secure maintenance payments, where it appears that:

1. the aggregate of the payments made for the purposes of the maintenance order by the debtor (whether under the AEO or otherwise) exceeds the aggregate of payments required up to that time by the maintenance order, and
2. the normal deduction rate exceeds the rate of payments required by the maintenance order, and
3. no proceedings for the variation or discharge of the attachment order are pending,

the clerk must apply to the court for the appropriate variation order. This is an order varying the AEO by reducing the NDR to the rate of the payments required to be made by the maintenance order, or such lower rate as the court thinks fit having regard to any excess payment (AEA 1971, s 10(1)). The court must grant such an application, unless the debtor appears and requests the court to discharge the order or to vary it in some other way, and the court thinks fit to grant the request. The clerk is required to give notice of the application to the person entitled to the payments under the maintenance order. The notice must be in writing setting out the time and place appointed for the hearing. The application is by way of complaint.

4. Discharge and variation in respect of persons residing outside England and Wales

A magistrates' court has jurisdiction to hear a complaint by or against a person residing outside England and Wales for the discharge or variation of an AEO made by a magistrates' court to secure maintenance payments (AEA 1971, s 20(1)).

Procedure is by way of complaint (AEA 1971, s 19(1)). If the defendant resides in Scotland or Northern Ireland, section 15 of the Maintenance Orders Act 1950 (which makes provision for the service of process on persons in those countries) will apply. Where the defendant resides outside the United Kingdom and does not appear at the time and place appointed for the hearing of the complaint, the court may, if it thinks it reasonable in all the circumstances, proceed to hear the complaint that party's absence, provided it is proved to the court's satisfaction that the complainant has taken steps to give notice to the defendant of the complaint and of the time and place appointed for hearing the complaint (1971 Rules, r 10(1) (2)). Any of the following steps, if proved to the court's satisfaction, will suffice:

1. The causing of written notice of the complaint and of the time and place appointed for the hearing to be delivered to the defendant.
2. The causing of written notice of the complaint and of the time and place appointed for the hearing to be sent by post, addressed to the defendant at his last known or usual place of abode, or at his place of business, or at some other address at which there is ground for believing that it will reach him.
3. The causing of notice of the complaint and of the time and place appointed for the hearing to be inserted in one or more newspapers on one or more occasions.

In relation to **1.** above, the Magistrates' Courts Rules 1981 apply for the purpose of proving delivery in the same way as they apply to prove service of a summons, with the addition that a declaration can also be made before a consular officer (Magistrates' Courts Rules 1981, r 67(1), as modified by the 1971 Rules, r 10(3)). However, in relation to **2.** or **3.** above, the complainant must first apply for directions to the court dealing with the complaint and the taking of such steps is only effective if they were taken in accordance with any directions given. Thereafter, any steps taken in relation to **2.** or **3.** can also be proved in accordance with the Magistrates' Courts Rules 1981.

5. Scotland and Northern Ireland

If the defendant resides in Scotland or Northern Ireland, any process issued must be endorsed, in Scotland by a sheriff, in Northern Ireland by a resident magistrate, and then served personally (Magistrates' Courts Rules 1981, r 67(1), as modified by the 1971 Rules, r 10(4)). Service can then be proved by means of declaration before either of the above endorsing authorities, as the case may be. It follows therefore that the steps at either **2.** or **3.** above, are not applicable (AEA 1971, s 20(2) and MOA 1950, s 15).

Whether a person is ordinarily resident is always a matter of fact and degree in each case (*R* v *Edgehill* [1963] 1 All ER 181).

6. Debtor not traced

Where a complaint by the debtor for the variation or discharge of an AEO is made against a person who does not appear at the time and place appointed for hearing the complaint then the court may, if it thinks it reasonable in all the circumstances, proceed to hear the complaint provided:

1. it is proved to the court's satisfaction that the summons was served in accordance with rule 99(1)(*b*) or (*c*) of the Magistrates' Courts Rules 1981; and
2. the complainant has caused notice of the complaint and of the time and place of the hearing to be inserted in one or more newspapers on one or more occasions (1971 Rules, r 11(1)(2)).

Application for directions must be made to the court before this procedure is used, and any other steps taken at **2.** are only effective if they comply with the directions given (Magistrates' Courts Rules 1981, r 67(2), as modified by the 1971 Rules, r 11(3)). Thereafter any steps taken can be proved in accordance with the Magistrates' Courts Rules 1981.

Lapse and discharge

1. Lapse

Where an order has been made and the employer ceases to have the debtor in his employment, the order lapses (except in regard to deductions from earnings paid after the cesser, and payment to the court of amounts deducted at any time) and is of no effect unless and until the court directs it to a person (whether the same as before or another) who appears to the court to have the debtor in his employment (AEA 1971, s 9(4)).

Should an order so lapse then if it appears to the court or justices' clerk that the debtor has subsequently entered the employment of a person (whether the same as before or another) the court may of its own motion vary the order by directing it to that person and may make any consequential amendment to the order (AEA 1971, s 9(3)(*a*); 1971 Rules, r 13). As the court proceeds by way of its own motion, no application is required.

The lapse of an order does not prevent its being treated as remaining in force for other purposes. This means for example, that a debtor commits an offence if, where an order has lapsed, he becomes re-employed, and fails to notify the court.

2. Discharge

Where it appears to a court or justices' clerk that the debtor is no longer employed, and that the likelihood of his entering the employment of any person is not such as to justify preserving the order, the court may, of its own motion discharge the order (1971 Rules, r 13). Where the court so discharges an order, the employer is under no liability in consequence of his treating it as still in force at any time before the expiration of seven days from the date on which a copy of the discharging order is served on him (AEA 1971, s 12(3)).

Power of court to determine whether payments are earnings

Where an order is in force, the court has power on application to decide whether payments to a debtor of a type specified in the application are earnings for the purposes of the order. The application to the court is by way of complaint. No form of complaint is prescribed. An application for such a determination may be made under section 16 of the AEA 1971 by:

- the employer;
- the debtor;
- the person to whom payment under the relevant adjudication is required to be made (whether directly or through an officer of any court).

Once a determination has been made an employer is entitled to give effect to it.

Where application has been made by an employer he does not incur any liability for non-compliance with the order in respect of any payments of the class specified in the application while the application or any appeal in consequence thereof is pending. This ceases to apply, unless the court otherwise directs, if the employer subsequently withdraws the application or abandons the appeal.

The court may make such order as it thinks just and reasonable for the payment by any of the parties to the application of the whole or any part of the costs of the determination (AEA 1971, s 21).

Consolidated orders

The power to make an AEO includes the power to make an order to secure the discharge of any number of relevant liabilities. An order made in this manner is known as a consolidated attachment of earnings order (AEA 1971, s 17(1)(2)). Thus, rather than make a number of orders, the court may instead make one consolidated order. This power is extended as follows:

1. in a case where the court has power to make an AEO in respect of a debtor who is already subject to such an order made by any magistrates' court, the court may discharge the existing order and make a consolidated order in respect of the debtor;
2. where two or more orders (whether or not themselves consolidated orders) made by magistrates' courts are in existence in respect of a debtor, any such court may discharge the existing orders and make a consolidated order.

A court is not, however, entitled under either **1.** or **2.** above to discharge an existing order made by another magistrates' court without first giving notice to the clerk of that court. In addition enforcement of the sum to which the other order related must first be transmitted to the court wishing to make the consolidated order. Transfer of enforcement in such circumstances may be by way of the normal provisions relating to transfer of fines (1971 Rules, r 16). Where a court wishes to make a consolidated order and the debtor does not reside within the petty sessions area for which that court acts, nor is within the area of the court which made the existing AEO, then the court which made the existing order may make an order transferring enforcement of the sum to which the order relates to the court wishing to make the consolidated order.

The power to make a consolidated order may be exercised by the court of its own motion or on the application of the debtor.

It is open to an employer to apply in writing to the clerk of the court which has power to make a consolidated order, requesting the clerk to make such an order (1971 Rules, r 15(7)). The clerk must then bring the application before the court. If it appears to the court that the application is justified, it proceeds as if it had determined of its own motion to make such an order.

Where the court proceeds by way of its own motion in a case to which **2.** above applies, the court must send written notice to the debtor informing him of his right to make representations to the court before it exercises its power (1971 Rules, r 15(8)).

The debtor's application for a consolidated order may be made at the hearing of the proceedings for the enforcement of the fine or other liability both where the court has power to make an original consolidated order and where this power is extended as in **1.** above. In cases to which **2.** applies, the debtor's application is by way of complaint.

Payments received under a consolidated order are to be applied first against sums previously secured by an AEO subsequently discharged in consequence of the making of the consolidated order (1971 Rules, r 17). Where two or more such AEOs have been discharged, the sums due under these orders must be paid off chronologically.

On making a consolidated order the court may set the NDR at such level as it thinks reasonable, which may be less than the sum of the NDR specified in the AEOs discharged by the court (1971 Rules, r 15(10)).

Cessation of order

An order ceases to have effect upon the issue of a warrant committing the debtor to prison for default in making the payment of the sums to which the order related (AEA 1971, s 8(5)). In the case of an order made to secure maintenance payments, the order ceases to have effect as follows:

1. on the making of an order of commitment or the issue of a commitment warrant in proceedings for enforcement of the maintenance order, and where the court postpones the issue of the commitment warrant in such proceedings;
2. upon the grant of an application for registration in a magistrates' court of a High Court or county court maintenance order, or upon the grant of an application for registration in the High Court of a magistrates' court maintenance order.
3. upon the discharge of the maintenance order while it is not registered as above, provided that where there remain arrears to be recovered after the maintenance order is discharged, the court discharging the order may direct that the AEO should not cease by virtue of the discharge of the related maintenance order.

Where an order ceases to have effect in such circumstances, notice of the cesser must be given to the employer by the clerk of the court which issued the warrant of commitment (AEA 1971, s 12(1) and 1971 Rules, r 21). A copy of the notice must be given to the county court registrar for the district in which the debtor resides. The employer is under no liability in consequence of his treating the order as still in force at any time before the expiration of seven days from the date on which the notice was served upon him.

Priority between orders

Where an employer has to comply with two or more orders made by a magistrates' court in respect of one debtor, then on any payday the employer, under paragraph 7 of Schedule 3 to the AEA 1971, must:

1. deal with the orders according to the dates on which they were made, disregarding any later one until an earlier one has been dealt with; and
2. deal with any later order as if the earnings to which it relates were the residue of a debtor's earnings after the making of any deduction to comply with any earlier order.

When one or more (but not all) of the orders have been made to secure payment of a judgement debt or administration order, then on any payday the employer, under paragraph 8 of schedule 3 to the AEA 1971 must:

1. deal first with any order made by a magistrates' court as above; and
2. deal thereafter with any order not made by a magistrates' court in the same way as orders made by magistrates' courts.

Service of orders and notices

Where a court makes an AEO or makes or discharges such an order, the clerk must ensure that a copy of the order is served upon the employer and the debtor (1971 Rules, r 6). A copy of the order must be given to the county court registrar for the district in which the debtor resides.

Any notice or order required to be served on the debtor may be served by delivering it to him personally, or by sending it by post to him at his last known or usual place of abode (1971 Rules, r 20). Any notice or order required to be served on the employer may be served, in the case of a corporation, by delivering the document or by sending to its registered office if this is in England or Wales. If other than a corporation, service may be effected at any place where the corporation trades or conducts its business, or by delivering or sending the document to such office or place as the corporation may have specified in writing to the court in relation to the debtor or in relation to a class or description to which he belongs. In the case of an employer who is not a corporation, service may be effected by delivering or sending the document to his place of business.

PART 7: ENFORCEMENT OF LEGAL AID CONTRIBUTIONS

CHAPTER 13

Enforcement of Legal Aid Contribution Orders

CHAPTER 13

Enforcement of Legal Aid Contribution Orders

Introduction

When an application for legal aid is made, contributions are assessed and prescribed figures for income and capital are taken into account in assessing a defendant's resources. Those with disposable income or capital levels below prescribed limits pay no contribution.

Where a contribution is ordered, it is to be paid in instalments from the date on which legal aid is granted. The instalments fall due weekly, but can be collected fortnightly or monthly should the court and the defendant find this more convenient.

The regulations also provide for re-assessment where an assisted person's resources change, and for consequent variation of the contribution order. If the assisted person wilfully refuses to pay instalments, the courts have power, during the proceedings, to revoke legal aid if satisfied that the assisted person could afford to pay at the time he fell into arrears and can currently afford to pay all or part of the sum. He must, however, have been given the opportunity to make representations against revocation. It may be preferable in certain cases to use the normal methods of enforcement at the end of the proceedings. At the conclusion of the case, the court before which the proceedings have been held has the power to remit any or all of the contribution instalments which have not fallen due, and to return contributions to acquitted defendants.

Recovery by the collecting court

Paragraph 2(1) of Schedule 3 to the Legal Aid Act 1988 (LAA 1988) provides that any sum ordered to be paid by way of a legal aid contribution order is recoverable by the collecting court as if it had been adjudged to be paid by an order of that court. "Collecting court" means a magistrates' court specified in the order, namely (LAA 1988, Sched 3, para 1):

1. where the court making the order is itself a magistrates' court, that court;
2. where the order is made on appeal from a magistrates' court, or in respect of a person against whom proceedings were transferred for trial or who was committed for sentence to the Crown Court, the court from which the appeal is brought or, as the case may be, which transferred the proceedings against him and committed him for sentence;
3. in any other case, a magistrates' court nominated by the court making the order.

Any provision made by the court which made the order as to time for payment, or payment by instalments, is treated as made by the collecting court.

Commencement of proceedings

Paragraph 6 of Schedule 3 of the LAA 1988 provides that any sum due under a legal aid contribution order cannot be recovered, and payment of any such sum cannot be enforced until either the conclusion of the relevant proceedings or if earlier, the revocation of the legal aid order in connection with which the legal aid contribution order was made.

Usually, however, the legal aid contribution order will not be enforced until the conclusion of the relevant proceedings. It will be rare for the court to revoke legal aid during the proceedings and enforce the contributions outstanding at the time of revocation.

Courts are advised to delay enforcing a contribution order until notification of the taxed costs is received from the taxing authority, in case repayment of any contribution in excess of the taxed costs is required. This can and does delay enforcement for several weeks.

Procedure for recovery

Various provisions apply as if a legal aid contribution order were enforceable as a magistrates' court maintenance order. They are examined in the previous chapter but for the sake of completeness the following is a brief summary of the essential provisions:

1. proceedings are begun by complaint;
2. a complaint must not be made earlier than the 15th day after the making of the order;

3. the court must not hear the complaint in the defendant's absence, unless it is proved to the court's satisfaction that the summons was served on him within a reasonable time before the hearing, or the defendant has previously appeared;
4. an attachment of earnings order can be made
5. a warrant may be issued for the defendant's arrest if the complaint is substantiated on oath;
6. instead of requiring immediate payment, the court can allow time for payment or order payment by instalments;
7. imprisonment for default must not be imposed unless the court has inquired, in the defendant's presence, whether the default was due to the defendant's wilful refusal or culpable neglect, and the court is of the opinion that it is so due;
8. imprisonment for default must not be imposed unless the court is of the opinion that it is inappropriate to make an attachment of earnings order;
9. imprisonment for default must not be imposed in the defendant's absence;
10. a commitment warrant must comply with Schedule 4 to the MCA 1980 regarding maximum periods of imprisonment, but in any event must not exceed six weeks;
11. imprisonment does not operate to discharge the defendant from liability to pay the sum for which he has been committed;
12. a defendant cannot be committed more than once for the same arrears;
13. any money found on the defaulter can be applied to satisfy the debt;
14. the court has the power to review committals, and the provisions of section 18 of the MOA 1958 apply as if the legal aid contribution order were a maintenance order;
15. the court has the power to remit arrears;
16. any costs awarded on the enforcement of a legal aid contribution order are enforceable as part of that order.

Transfer of enforcement proceedings to a different court

Where it appears to the collecting court that a person subject to a legal aid contribution order is residing in another petty sessions area, it may make an order making payments under the legal aid contribution order enforceable in that other petty sessions area. This order is referred to as a "transfer order" (LAA 1988, Sched 3, para 5).

Members of the armed forces

Where a legal aid contribution order has been made against a member of the armed forces and deductions are being made by the Secretary of State from that person's pay, the court cannot enforce the order unless and until the Secretary of State has notified the court that the person is no longer a member of the forces (LAA 1988, Sched 3, para 7).

Recovery in the High Court or county court

A legal aid contribution order is enforceable in the High Court or county court (otherwise than by issue of a writ of fieri facias or other process against goods, or by imprisonment, or attachment of earnings) as if the sum were due to the collecting court clerk by a judgement or order of the High Court or county court (LAA 1988, Sched 3, para 3). However, no proceedings for recovery may be taken in the High Court or county court by the clerk unless he is authorised to do so by the court.

Power to defer enforcement proceedings

The collecting court may defer recovering the sum under a contribution order if an appeal is pending in respect of the proceedings for which legal aid was granted; or the person granted representation has been ordered to be retried (LAA 1988, Sched 3, para 8).

PART 8: ENFORCEMENT OF CIVIL DEBT

CHAPTER 14

Civil Debt

CHAPTER 14

Civil Debt

Introduction

Rather confusingly the subject of civil debt is divided into two areas; those sums which are *recoverable* as a civil debt, and those which are *enforceable* as a civil debt.

Sums recoverable as a civil debt

1. Generally

A magistrates' court has power, on complaint, to make an order for the payment of any money recoverable summarily as a civil debt. Any sum ordered by a magistrates' court is recoverable summarily as a civil debt, except the following (MCA 1980, s58(1)(2)):

- i) a sum recoverable on complaint for a magistrates' court maintenance order; or
- ii) a sum that may be adjudged to be paid by a summary conviction or by an order enforceable as if it were a summary conviction.

2. Procedure

Application is by complaint to the court which has jurisdiction in the area where the act was either done or left undone (in this case where the debt is payable) and the defendant is to be summoned (MCA 1980, ss 51 and 52). Complaint must be made within six months from the time the matter of complaint arose, namely when the debt became due (MCA 1980, s 127), but note the 12-month time limit allowed for the recovery of any tax charged under Schedule E (Taxes Management Act 1970, s 65(3))

Form 104 1981 in the Magistrates' Court (Forms) Rules is the prescribed form.

3. Hearing

On hearing the complaint, the substance of it is to be stated to the defendant if he appears. After hearing the evidence and the parties, the court must make the order or dismiss the complaint. With the defendant's consent the court may make the order without hearing the evidence (MCA 1980, s 53(3)). Otherwise the order of evidence and speeches is as prescribed by Magistrates' Court Rules 1981.

Procedures regarding adjournments and non-appearance of either the defendant or the complainant are governed by the general provisions contained in Part II of the MCA 1980 relating to civil jurisdiction and procedure, in particular section 54 (adjournments); section 55 (non-appearance of defendant); section 56 (non-appearance of complainant); and 57 (non-appearance of both parties). The court, however, is precluded from issuing a warrant for the defendant's arrest if he fails to appear (section 55(8)).

4. The order

A sum "recoverable as a civil debt" simply means a sum which has not yet been, but may be, ordered to be paid; the order therefore is for payment of the debt. All the court has to satisfy itself is that the debt is indeed a civil debt, and that it is owed by the defendant. Any question of wilful refusal or culpable neglect is irrelevant. However, the court is not obliged to make the order and could, with good cause, decline to do so. For example, a bankruptcy or administration order may be good cause. However, a bankruptcy notice (now a statutory demand under section 268 of the Insolvency Act 1986) may be founded on the making of a civil debt order (*Re A Debtor (No 48 of 1952), ex parte Ampthill Rural District Council* v *The Debtor* [1953] 1 All ER 545). Form 106 in the Magistrates' Courts (Forms) Rules 1981 is the prescribed form of order. The court may order immediate payment of the money or allow payment by instalments; it may even allow further time to pay (MCA 1980, s 75).

Default by the defendant in paying one instalment renders the whole amount enforceable. In *Abley* v *Dale* (1851) 15 JP 147 and *ex parte Kinning* (1847) 10 QB 730 it was suggested that where time for payment is allowed in relation to the payment of a civil debt, then before further process is issued for the enforcement of such a debt, the defendant should be given the opportunity of being heard. The principle appears to be that, notwithstanding the defendant's non-payment, circumstances might possibly occur between the making of the order and the time of imprisoning the defendant which would cause the judge not to commit him. In ex parte Kinning, Maule J said: "suppose, for instance, the man were in the last stage of cholera when the time for payment arrives; should he not have an opportunity of making that fact known to the judge before being committed for non-payment".

While accepting that in the 1990s it would be rare for a defendant to be "in the last stage of cholera" the principle behind the judgment is still as relevant. The very object of the order is to make the payments subject to all the contingencies which may happen at a future time. As a rule of practice, if nothing else, it is strongly suggested that a summons should be issued before further action is taken.

5. Reserve and auxiliary forces

Protection is available to members of the reserve and auxiliary forces. Leave to proceed may be required in accordance with the Reserve and Auxiliary Forces (Protection of Civil Interests) Rules 1951 (SI No 1401).

6. Costs

Costs are payable at the court's discretion in such amount as it thinks just and reasonable (s64(1) MCA 1980), but the complainant's costs can only be paid on making the order for which the complaint is made. Similarly, the defendant's costs can only be paid on dismissing the complaint.

Costs ordered to be paid are enforceable as a civil debt (MCA 1980, s 64(4)).

Sums enforceable as a civil debt

A sum enforceable as a civil debt is defined by section 150 of the MCA 1980 as:

1. any sum recoverable summarily as a civil debt *which is adjudged to be paid by the order of a magistrates' court*;
2. any other sum expressed by the MCA 1980 or any other Act to be so enforceable.

In the case of **2.** above, no "civil debt order" made as a result of civil debt proceedings is required before enforcement is commenced. For example, costs ordered in civil proceedings under section 64 of the MCA 1980 (subject to exceptions) are described as being "enforceable as a civil debt". See also Part II of Schedule 9 to the Administration of Justice Act 1970.

The powers available to the court in enforcing civil debt are distress (available in all cases) or imprisonment (restricted to a very few cases).

Distress

A distress warrant is not to be issued for failure to pay a sum of money enforceable as a civil debt unless, rule 53 of the Magistrates' Courts Rules 1981:

1. a copy of the minute of the order has been served by delivering it to the defendant or by sending it to him by post at his last known or usual place of abode; or
2. the order was made in his presence and the warrant issued on that occasion

Imprisonment

1. Generally

The Administration of Justice Act 1970 severely restricted the magistrates' powers to commit for civil debt. Under Schedule 4 to the 1970 Act, they can now only commit in relation to orders for the payment of the following:

1. income tax or any other tax liability recoverable under section 65, 66 or 68 of the Taxes Management Act 1970;
2. State Scheme premiums under Part III of the Pension Schemes Act 1993;
3. Class 1, 2 and 4 contributions under Part I of the Social Security, Contributions and Benefits Act 1992

Restrictions in relation to the custody of young persons (aged 18–20) imposed by section 9 of the Criminal Justice Act 1982 (as amended by the CJA 1991) are also applicable (MCA 1980, s 96A).

2. Procedure

Application is by complaint and can be made at any time, notwithstanding the normal six months' time limitation (MCA 1980, s 96).

Proceedings for the summary recovery of any tax due will be commenced in the name of a collector and proceedings begun by one collector may be continued by another (Taxes Management Act 1970, s 1(3)). All or any of the sums due in respect of tax from any one person and payable to any one collector may, whether or not they are due under one assessment, be included in the same complaint, summons, order, warrant or other document; and every such document shall be construed as a single document as respects each sum (Taxes Management Act 1970, s 65(2)).

The summons is known as a "judgment summons" and must be served on the judgment debtor personally (Magistrates' Court Rules 1981, r 58). However, if a Justice of the Peace is satisfied by evidence on oath that prompt personal service is impracticable he may allow the summons to be served in such a way as he thinks just in the circumstances of that particular case. Service of the summons outside the commission area can be proved by affidavit, although the Summary Jurisdiction (Process) Act 1881 (Service of Process in Scotland) does not apply to the recovery of civil debts. Forms 107 and 108 in the Magistrates' Court (Forms) Rules 1981 are the prescribed forms of complaint and summons.

Where the summons was served less than three clear days before the hearing, the court may not hear the complaint unless the judgment debtor actually appears and consents to an immediate hearing.

If the defendant fails to appear at the time and place appointed for the hearing, the court can proceed in his absence (MCA 1980, s55(1)(8)). A warrant cannot be issued for the debtor's arrest in proceedings for the enforcement of a sum recoverable summarily as a civil debt, nor can a warrant for the arrest of a witness (ie the debtor) be issued as an indirect method of procuring attendance (MCA 1980, s 97(2)).

3. The hearing

Under section 96(1) of the MCA 1980, the complainant must prove to the court's satisfaction that:

1. the judgment debtor has, or has had since the date on which the sum was adjudged to be paid, the means to pay the sum, or any instalment of it on which he has defaulted; and
2. he refuses or neglects, or has refused or neglected to pay it

While the court is under no statutory obligation to consider all other methods, it must surely be the case that imprisonment is to be used only as a last resort where no other method is appropriate. Where there is a reasonable likelihood that the debtor has assets available to satisfy the debt it is submitted that the justices should proceed by way of distress rather than by commitment.

The court has no power to make a money payment supervision order or remit any part of the civil debt.

4. Period of imprisonment

The maximum periods applicable are those contained in Schedule 4 to the MCA 1980 but must not in any event exceed six weeks. Postponement of the warrant is possible but it may not be issued, it is submitted, without giving the defendant the right to be heard, in line with the enforcement of other debts.

5. Payment after imprisonment imposed

On payment of the full debt together with costs (if any) the commitment will cease to have effect, and the defendant will be released unless he is in custody for some other cause (MCA 1980, s 79(1)).

Where payment is made of only part of the sum due, this will have the effect of reducing the period of detention proportionately. The persons authorised to receive part payment after imprisonment has been imposed are prescribed by rule 55(1) of the Magistrates' Court Rules 1981.

6. Attachment of earnings

There is no provision for a magistrates' court to make an attachment of earnings order in relation to civil debt (AEA 1971, s 1). However, the county court can make such order to secure the payment of a judgment debt of not less than £5. This would include a magistrates' court order which is enforceable as a civil debt (AEA 1971, s 2).

7. Costs

The court may order the debtor to pay such costs as it thinks just and reasonable (MCA 1980, s 64). Where the defendant is committed to custody, such costs incurred by the complainant as the court may direct shall be included in the sum on payment of which the defendant may be released from custody (MCA 1980, s 96(3)).

PART 9: ENFORCEMENT OF COMMUNITY CHARGE AND COUNCIL TAX

CHAPTER 15

Enforcement of Community Charge and Council Tax

CHAPTER 15

Enforcement of Community Charge and Council Tax

Introduction

The enforcement of both community charge and council tax follows the same basic framework. Local authorities wishing to recover outstanding payments may apply to magistrates' courts for a "liability order" which empowers the charging authorities to recover the outstanding payments by a number of different methods; ultimately if these methods fail, the local authority may then apply to the magistrates' court for committal to prison for non-payment.

Service of notices

Before the court may grant a liability order, the local authority must satisfy the court that the statutory notices have been served as required.

1. Community charge

The local authority is required to serve notices in accordance with the Community Charges (Administration and Enforcement) Regulations 1989 (the 1989 Regulations). The requirements to serve notices depends upon the method of payment adopted and whether recovery is in respect of the personal, standard or collective community charge. In each case however the local authority is required to serve a demand notice. Where there is a failure to pay, the local authority must adopt the following procedure under Parts III and IV of the 1989 Regulations:

Failure to pay instalments under the statutory. instalment scheme in Schedule 1: personal and standard community charge Where a demand notice has been served and where an instalment has been missed the local authority must serve a further notice stating the instalments required to be paid. Where payments are not made within the period of seven days beginning with the day of service of the further notice, then the whole amount owing for the year becomes payable within a further period of seven days. Once the notice has been served and the 14-day period has expired, the local authority may bring proceedings in a magistrates' court for a liability order for the amount outstanding for the year.

Failure to pay instalments under the statutory instalment scheme in Schedule 2 or submit a return: collective community charge
The provisions are, in effect, identical in that where a demand notice has been served and an instalment has been missed the unpaid balance of the charge becomes payable on the day after the end of the period of 14 days beginning with the day of the failure. However, before making application for a liability order the local authority is required to serve a notice specifying the amount due and requiring payment within a period of seven days. Once the seven-day period has elapsed and payment has not been made, then the local authority may make application for a liability order.

Payments by separate agreement: personal and standard charge and collective community charge Where a demand notice has been served and where the local authority has agreed to a method of payment other than the statutory instalment scheme and payments are not made as agreed, the local authority before making application or a liability order must serve a reminder notice. The reminder notice may be served in respect of an amount at any time after it has become due and if it is not paid by the expiry of the period of seven days beginning with the day on which the notice was served, the local authority may apply to a magistrates' court for a liability order. The amount stated in the reminder notice in these circumstances is the amount owing at the time and not the full balance outstanding for the year. It is only where payments are made by instalments in accordance with the statutory instalment scheme and the payment is missed that the balance for the year becomes payable, unless the agreement itself makes provision for the full amount to become due once one instalment is missed.

Payments in a single amount: personal and standard charge and collective community charge Where payment is required after the year end, for example where a final adjustment has been made and the amount required to be paid for the year is greater than estimated, the local authority must serve a further notice allowing a period of not less than 14 days for payment. Where payment is not made within the 14 days the local authority may then issue a reminder notice; if the amount is not paid within a further period of seven days beginning with the day on which the notice was served, then the local authority may apply for a liability order in respect of that amount.

2. Council Tax

There is a similar requirement imposed upon the local authority to serve notices imposed by the Council Tax (Administration and Enforcement) Regulations 1992 (the 1992 Regulations). The requirements differ depending upon the method of payment adopted. Again, the local authority is required to serve a demand notice on every liable person. Where there is a failure to pay the local authority must adopt the following procedure to be found in Parts V and VI of the 1992 Regulations:

Payment by instalments under the statutory instalment scheme in Schedule 1 Where a demand notice has been served and an instalment has been missed, the local authority is required to serve a reminder notice stating that unless payment of the amounts due is made within the next seven days then the total amount outstanding for the year will be due within a further period of seven days. Where two reminder notices are issued within the same year and on each occasion the payments are brought up to date, if there is a third default there is no requirement to serve a further notice and the whole amount due for the year becomes payable, provided that the previous reminder notice explained the consequences of a further failure.

Other payment methods Where payments are not made in accordance with the statutory instalment schemes or where a demand notice is served after the end of the year to which it relates (in which case at least 14 days must be allowed for payment) then the local authority is required to serve a final notice setting out the amount due. Where the amount is unpaid at the end of the period of seven days beginning with the day on which the notice was issued, the local authority may apply to a magistrates' court for a liability order. The amount due to be paid is the amount outstanding at the time, not the amount due for the year, unless the agreement itself provides otherwise.

Service of notices Notices served under the 1989 and 1992 Regulations may be served in accordance with the provisions of section 233 of the Local Government Act 1972. These provisions allow notice to be served or given to a liable person by delivering it to him, or by leaving it at his proper address, or by sending it by post to him at that address. Any notice may, in the case of a body corporate, be given to or served on the secretary or clerk of that body and, in the case of a partnership, be given to or served on a partner or a person having the control or management of the partnership business. The proper address of any person to be given or served with a notice is his last known address except, in the case of a body corporate, it is the address of the registered or principal office and, in the case of a partnership, it is the principal office of the partnership.

Application for a liability order The same procedure applies whether application is made for the recovery of outstanding community charge or outstanding council tax. The application is instituted by making complaint to a Justice of the Peace and requesting the issue of a summons directing a person to appear before the court to show why he has not paid the sum outstanding. The application must be made within six years of the day on which the amount became due. The court has no power to issue a warrant, but must proceed by way of summons only.

The court must make the order if it is satisfied that the sum has become payable by the defendant and has not been paid. The court has no discretion and must make the order in the sum payable, provided that the notices have been served as required by the statutory provisions. In *R* v *Bristol City Council, ex parte Willsman and another* (1991) 156 JP 409 the Court of Appeal held that a local authority was not prevented from seeking a liability order against a community charge payer before determining that person's claim for community charge benefit. This was the case even where the local authority was in breach of its statutory duty to determine a claim to benefit within the period prescribed by the regulations.

The local authority may also make application for costs reasonably incurred in obtaining the order. Here, the court may exercise its discretion in determining what amount is reasonable, but where the sum owing is paid after a liability order has been applied for but before it is made, the court is obliged, if so requested by the local authority to award the costs reasonably incurred by that authority when making the application.

The summons may be served by one of the following methods:

1. by delivering it to him personally,
2. by leaving it at his usual or last known place of residence, or in the case of a company at its registered office, or
3. by sending it by post to him at his usual or last known place of residence, or in the case of a company, to its registered office, or
4. by leaving it at, or by sending it by post to him at, an address given by that person as an address at which service of the summons will be accepted.

The Hearing

Justices of the Peace acting for the commission area within which the local authority is situated have jurisdiction to act both under the 1989 and the 1992 Regulations. The court must be composed of at least two justices except where a stipendiary magistrate is sitting.

1. Conduct of the proceedings

The community charge or council tax defaulter may appear in person or may be legally represented. A defaulter may wish to seek the assistance of a "McKenzie friend". In *R* v *Leicester City Justices, ex parte Barrow and another* [1991] 3 All ER 935 it was held by the Court of Appeal that the court's administration of justice had not only to be fair, but to be seen to be so. A party appearing in person should therefore be given reasonable assistance in conducting his case including that of an advisor, unless the court, in the exercise of its jurisdiction to maintain order and regulate proceedings before it, ordered otherwise. It was also held that the title "McKenzie friend" was better not used, and that such a person should more appropriately be referred to simply as an assistant or friend. In the course of the judgement Lord Donaldson, Master of the Rolls held that it was not correct to say that if the applicant were to be assisted by an assistant or friend, it could only be by express permission of the court; the position was that they could be assisted by him if the court did not rule otherwise. He agreed that the justices have inherent and statutory power to maintain order and regulate the proceedings before them. He also said that the clerk's role in both advising the magistrates of the law and seeking to assist a litigant in person was a very difficult one and that without in any way criticising justices' clerks, the applicants could reasonably seek other assistance. The fact that the issues were simple and straightforward was not relevant. Unless there were clear grounds in the interest of the proper administration of justice for denying them the assistance of an assistant or friend, it was enough that they should have thought that they needed it.

2. Legal aid

There is no right to legal aid in proceedings for enforcement of community charge or council tax. A decision is awaited from the European Court of Human Rights in *Benham* v *UK*. It is anticipated that the court will find that the proceedings for committal to prison were unlawful in light of the absence of any right to legal aid.

3. Civil proceedings

Proceedings for the recovery of unpaid community charge or council tax are not criminal proceedings and this was confirmed in *R* v *Highbury Corner Justices, ex parte Watkins* (1992) *The Times*, 22 October where it was held that since failure to pay the poll tax was not a criminal offence, the privilege which allowed a person to refuse to answer questions which might be self-incriminatory did not attach to questions put by justices to establish the payer's means as part of the procedure for enforcing the payment of poll tax. The evidential privilege against self incrimination had no relevance to questions being asked in civil proceedings for the recovery of unpaid tax.

4. Proof of liability — evidence: computer records: admissibility

In 1991 a stipendiary magistrate refused an application by Camden London Borough Council for liability orders on the basis that computerised records were not admissible to prove that payments had not been made. As a result of this case the Community Charges Regulations 1989 were amended and identical provisions have been incorporated into the Council Tax Regulations 1992. It is now provided that in any proceedings for an application for a liability order or an application for commitment to prison or in relation to an appeal in connection with distress, a statement contained in a document constituting or forming part of a record compiled by the applicant authority shall be admissible as evidence of any fact stated in it of which direct oral evidence would be admissible. Where the document containing the statement is produced by a computer, it is admissible as evidence of anything stated in it to the best of the signatory's information and belief provided that a certificate is produced which:

1. identifies the document containing the statement and the computer by which it was produced;
2. contains a statement that at all material times the computer was operating properly, or if not, that any respect in which it was not operating properly or was out of operation was not such as to affect the production of the document or the accuracy of its contents;
3. gives such explanation as may be appropriate of the document's content; and
4. purports to be signed by a person occupying a responsible position in relation to the operation of the computer.

1. Community charge

The local authority must show that:

1. the community charge was fixed by resolution of the authority,
2. the defaulter's name was entered in a community charges register of the authority,
3. the community charge was demanded in accordance with the statutory provisions,
4. payment of the charge had not been made by the due date,
5. reminder or final notices were served in accordance with the statutory provisions,
6. the full amount due (including costs) has not been paid.

The court has no discretion in that it must make the order if it is satisfied that the sum has become payable by the defaulter and has not been paid.

2. Council tax

The local authority must show that:

1. the council tax was fixed by resolution of the authority;
2. the defendant is liable to the council tax;
3. council tax is payable in respect to the dwelling;
4. the council tax has been demanded in accordance with the statutory provisions;
5. payment of the council tax had not been made by the due date;
6. reminder notices and final notices have been served in accordance with the statutory provisions; and
7. the full amount due (including costs) has not been paid.

Again the court has no discretion in that it must make the order if it is satisfied that the sum has become payable by the defaulter and has not been paid.

Powers under a liability order

The enforcement provisions are to be found in Part IV of the 1989 Regulations and Part VI of the 1992 Regulations.

1. Duties of debtors subject to liability order

Where a liability order has been made the debtor is under a duty to supply relevant information to the authority during such time as the amount in respect of the order was made remains wholly or partly unpaid.

2. Attachment of earnings order

Where an order has been made against a person who appears to be an individual, the authority may make an order to secure payment of any outstanding sum in respect of which the liability order was made. The local authority may serve a copy of the order on the employer, who is then under a duty to comply with it.

Regulations prescribe the sums to be deducted by the employer and also provide for the situation where an employee may be subject to more than one attachment of earnings order.

3. Attachment of allowances order

This order, available only under the 1992 Regulations, is similar in effect to an attachment of earnings order, but relates to an elected member of a billing authority or a major precepting authority.

4. Attachment of state benefits

Regulations provide for the local authority to apply to the Secretary of State asking him to deduct sums from income support payments made in order to secure the payment of any outstanding sum for which the liability order was made

5. Distress

Where a liability order has been made, the authority may levy the appropriate amount by distress and sale of the goods of the debtor against whom the order was made. The regulations provide for certain categories of goods which may not be seized. There is also provision in the regulations for a debtor to pay the amount owing before the goods are seized, and also to pay the amount owing (including any charges) after the goods have been seized but before the goods have been sold.

There is a procedure by which a person aggrieved by the levy of an amount by distress may appeal to a magistrates' court. The appeal is by way of complaint and if the court is satisfied that the levy was irregular, it may order the goods distrained to be discharged if they are in the possession of the authority or it may award compensation in respect of any goods distrained and sold. In the case of *R* v *Basildon Justices, ex parte Holding and Barnes plc* (1994) 158 JP 1980 it was held that where a levy, or an attempted levy of distress is challenged by way of an appeal to a magistrates' court (in this case under the Non-Domestic Rating (Collection and Enforcement) (Local Lists) Regulations 1989) and the court forms the opinion that the case will raise complex issues of title, the court has a discretion to decline to deal with the matter and leave the appellant to pursue alternative remedies in the county court or High Court.

6. Insolvency

The Regulations provide that where a liability order has been made the amount due under that order shall be deemed to be a debt for the purposes of bankruptcy and winding-up proceedings under the Insolvency Act 1986.

7. Charging orders

The regulations provide for a charging order to be applied for where a liability order has been made in respect of the collective community charge or where a liability order has been made in respect of council tax.

8. Commitment to prison

Where the authority has sought to levy an amount by distress and the person making the distress reports to the authority that he was unable (for whatever reason) to find any or sufficient goods of the debtor on which to levy the amount, the authority may apply to the magistrates' court for the issue of a warrant committing the debtor to prison.

The Regulations provide that where an application is made

> *"the court shall (in the debtor's presence) inquire as to his means and inquire whether the failure to pay ... was due to his wilful refusal or culpable neglect. If (and only if) the court is of the opinion that his failure was due to his wilful refusal or culpable neglect it may if it thinks fit—*
>
> *(a) issue a warrant of commitment against the debtor, or*
>
> *(b) fix a term of imprisonment and postpone the issue of a warrant until such time and on such conditions (if any) as the court thinks just."*

The local authority may make application in the warrant for a sum of an amount equal to the costs reasonably incurred by them in respect of the application.

The power to commit to prison must be exercised carefully, with due regard to the statutory provisions and to the substantial body of case law which has arisen following the enactment of these provisions. It is clear that the purpose of the power to commit to prison is to extract payment; it is not intended as a punishment and courts which proceed on the basis that it is a punishment will be criticised.

Notice of hearing The court is required to hold a means inquiry with the debtor present to determine whether his failure to pay was due to his wilful refusal or culpable neglect. Where the court holds such a means inquiry, but postpones the issue of the commitment warrant subject to conditions, and there is a breach of those conditions, the debtor must be given notice of a hearing at which a decision is made to commit him to prison, but there is no requirement that he must also be present at that hearing. This was the decision in *R* v *Northampton Justices, ex parte Newell* (1992) 157 JP 869 which approved the decision of *R* v *Faversham and Sittingbourne Magistrates' Court, ex parte Ursell* (1992) 156 JP 765 where it was said that natural justice required that notice of the hearing must be given to the debtor to give him the opportunity to be heard, but provided the debtor was properly notified, then there was no additional requirement that he must be present at the hearing at which the committal order was ordered to be issued. The court must be satisfied that notice has been given and delivered before issuing the committal warrant. Given that the requirement to serve notice is non-statutory, a notice served in accordance with the provisions of section 233 of the Local Government Act 1972 may not be sufficient to satisfy the requirement that notice has been given. The court may wish to hear that the notice has been served personally in the absence of any acknowledgement by the defaulter himself.

Preconditions to application for commitment warrant Application for commitment to prison may only be made where the authority has sought to levy an amount by distress and the person making the distress reports to the authority that he was unable to find any or sufficient goods on which to levy the amount. It was however held in the case of *R* v *Wolverhampton Magistrates' Court* (1992) 157 JP 1017 that when seeking a warrant of commitment for non-payment of community charge, the local authority need not produce evidence to establish the existence of the antecedent requirements set out in the Regulations.

Finding of wilful refusal or culpable neglect The 1989 Regulations require that the court determine whether a debtor's failure to pay at *the time the liability order was issued* was due to his wilful refusal or culpable neglect. As a first step therefore the court must establish when the liability order was issued and examine the circumstances from the date of the demand notice to the date when the liability order was made. The 1992 regulations, on the other hand require the court to inquire whether the failure to pay *which has led to the application (for committal)* is due to his wilful refusal or culpable neglect. There is the need for a wide inquiry therefore from the date of the demand to the date of the application for committal. To this extent the Regulations differ; otherwise the Regulations are drafted in similar, if not in identical, terms. Cases decided under the 1989 Regulations may therefore be relied upon when considering the 1992 Regulations.

The court is obliged to conduct a means inquiry and it is clear from the case of *R* v *Wolverhampton Stipendiary Magistrate, ex parte Mould* (1992) Rating Appeals 309 that a community charge debtor has a part to play in the proceedings other than the mere giving of evidence. It was said in that case that the stipendiary magistrate's failure to understand that point led to his unsustainable conclusion that the defaulter's request for the assistance of a friend should be refused. The court said the debtor might well have a part going beyond simply giving evidence; he might wish to challenge the evidence given by the charging authority as to his indebtedness and any steps taken by them to levy distress, or he may wish to challenge the information given about his means, or to submit that the failure to pay was not due to wilful refusal or culpable neglect or even if it was, that a commitment warrant, postponed on suitable conditions, was to be preferred to immediate custody.

The court is not obliged to give reasons for ordering immediate imprisonment but it was said in the case of *R* v *Wolverhampton Magistrates' Court* that it was desirable that reasons should be given for ordering the immediate imprisonment of a person entitled to the benefit of statutory restrictions on imprisoning young offenders under section 1(5) of the CJA 1982. Those particular provisions were discussed in the case of *R* v *Grimsby Justices, ex parte Hogg* (1994) 158 JP 1053 where it was held that the provisions applied when the commitment warrant was ordered to take effect and not when the original suspended committal order was made.

Courts have been held to have fallen into error where for example justices found that an unemployed person's failure to pay his community charge was due to culpable neglect because he had the potential to earn money when there was no clear evidence that employment had been on offer and that he had refused it (*R* v *Poole Justices, ex parte Benham* (1991) 156 JP 177).

In *R* v *Ramsgate Magistrates' Court and Another, ex parte Haddow* (1992) 157 JP 545 the court committed Mrs Haddow to prison for 14 days for failing to pay her community charge. The court made a finding of wilful refusal to pay and took into account the fact that a previous court had fixed a term of imprisonment against her husband, had postponed the issue of the warrant on condition that he make regular payments that he had failed to make those payments and had ultimately been committed to prison. The court concluded that Mrs Haddow had also decided to take a deliberate stance in not paying the community charge, knowing of the possible consequences. The magistrates were supported on appeal and it was said that the court was justified in concluding that a family decision had been taken not to pay and the husband's conduct was a material factor to which they were entitled to have regard. In this case the evidence supported the court's decision.

There is no statutory requirement for the court to try or consider all other methods of payment. Nevertheless, the court might be criticised if it did not consider the available alternatives to imprisonment to recover the money due. But as the case of *R* v *Felixstowe and Ipswich Borough Council, ex parte Herridge* (1993) Rating Appeals 83 makes clear payments of £2 per week available from deductions from income support was not an alternative where the court took the view that the defendant could pay £10 per week. And it was repeated in *R* v *Preston Justices, ex parte McCosh* (1995) *The Times,* 30 January that justices were not obliged to exhaust all possibilities of recovering unpaid community charge before making a suspended committal order.

It was accepted in *R* v *Felixstowe and Ipswich Borough Council* that the court must have the ultimate sanction to commit where a debtor had breached the conditions of a postponed committal order and that the court did not have to review the findings of a previous court when dealing with an application to issue a postponed warrant. However, where the court was invited to reconsider the basis upon which the previous court had proceeded on the grounds that the court made the wrong assumptions, then the court should not fetter its discretion by refusing to consider the matter. *R* v *Northampton Justices, ex parte Newell*. The court must in any event be satisfied that the debtor had the ability to pay under the postponed order, before issuing the commitment warrant.

Term The maximum term for which the debtor may be imprisoned is three months. The Regulations make provision for the number of days to be reduced following part-payment. Schedule 4 to the MCA 1980 does not apply but in *R* v *Highbury Corner Magistrates' Court, ex parte Uchendu* (1994) 158 JP 409 it was held that where a court was considering an application for committal to prison (in this instance for failure to pay non-domestic rates), the court must observe the principle of proportionality in the sense that the period of imprisonment should increase with the seriousness of the case, whether in terms of the amount outstanding, or the degree of culpability to be attached to the rate-payer for his non-payment. The court also held that it was less serious to fail to pay rates through culpable neglect than through wilful refusal.

Warrant Where a warrant is issued then it must be in the form specified in the 1989 Regulations (Form C in Schedule 3) or the 1992 Regulations (Form C in Schedule 2) or a form to the like effect.

Remission Where an application is made for committal but no warrant is issued or term of imprisonment fixed, the court may remit all or part of the sum with respect to which the application related. However, the court does not have an inherent power to remit once a term of imprisonment has been fixed or a warrant of commitment has been issued (*Harrogate Borough Council* v *Barker* (1995), The Times, 2nd June.

Renewal of application Where an application is made but no warrant issued or term of imprisonment fixed, the Regulations allow the application to be renewed on the ground that the debtor's circumstances have changed.

9. Relationship between remedies

Where a liability order has been made against a person the local authority may use only one method of recovery at a time, and that includes an application under the income support regulations which is undetermined. Attachment of allowances order, attachment of earnings order, distress or deductions from income support may be resorted to more than once and in any order

Where a commitment warrant is issued or a term of imprisonment fixed, no steps or no further steps may be taken by way of attachment of allowances (council tax only), attachment of earnings, distress, bankruptcy or charging or under the income support regulations in relation to the amount for which the warrant has been issued or the term of imprisonment fixed.

APPENDIX I
Giving Reasons

Where the court decides to commit, it will have gone through a reasoning process. The reasons for the court's decision must be set out in the warrant of commitment and in the court register. If not, there is a real likelihood that the commitment order will be quashed (*In re Cawley and Others,* 1996 160 JP 133).

The following must be specified:

1. The grounds for commitment, i.e.

   a) The defaulter is already serving a sentence of custody or detention.
   b) In the case of an offence punishable with imprisonment, that the defaulter appears to have sufficient means to pay forthwith.
   c) The default is due to the offender's wilful refusal or culpable neglect and the court has considered or tried all other methods of enforcing payment and they are inappropriate or unsuccessful.

2. When the committal order is based on the offender's wilful refusal or culpable neglect, the reasons for rejecting each of the other methods of enforcing payment available to the court.
3. Where the offender is under 21 years of age, the reason for finding that it is undesirable to place him under supervision (if no supervision order has been made).
4. Where the offender is under 21 years of age the reasons why no other method of dealing with him is appropriate otherwise than by detention in default of payment.

APPENDIX 2

Forms

Enforcement of fines etc.

Fixed penalties

Enforcement of maintenance orders

Attachment of earnings

APPENDIX 2

Forms

Enforcement of fines, etc

[All forms are in the Magistrates' Courts (Forms) Rules 1981 unless otherwise indicated.]

1. Notice of fine (Form 46)

	.... Magistrates' Court (Code)
	Date ....
	Case No ....
	Convicted on ....*(date)*.......... by the [............ Magistrates' Court] [Crown Court at ....]
	Driving Licence No ....

Offences	*Fine*	*Compen-sation*	*Costs*	*Total*
	£	£	£	£

You have been ordered to pay the sums shown above [by (*date*)] [by weekly/monthly instalments of £ the first instalment to be paid by (*date*)]

Payment may be made personally at the address shown below on (*days* between (*time*) and (*time*)); or—

By post to the address shown below, Crossed cheques and postal orders should be made payable to the 'Justices' Clerk'. Cash should not be sent in unregistered envelopes. Any communication sent by post must be properly stamped.

Payment to The Justices' Clerk
(Address)

(Telephone No)

Failure to pay in accordance with the above directions may result in a distress warrant being issued against you or a warrant for your arrest unless you have been granted further time for payment; application for further time for payment may be made in writing to the Justices' Clerk stating the grounds for the application.

NOTE: This notice should be sent with any payment or application.

2. Distress warrant (Form 48)

MAGISTRATES' COURT (Code)

Date:

Accused:

Address:

Offence	*Fine*	*Compensation*	*Costs*	*Total*
	£	£	£	£

was on (date) at [Crown Court] [Magistrates' Court] ordered to pay the sums specified above in accordance with the terms of the notice of fine served on the accused and default has been made in payment and the following sum is still outstanding:

Total amount £

*Still outstanding:**

Direction: You [the Constables of Police Force] [ ] are hereby required immediately to make distress of the money and goods of the accused (except the clothing and bedding of the accused and the accused's family, and to the value of fifty pounds, the tools and implements of the accused's trade); and if the amount shown above as still outstanding, together with the costs and charges of taking and keeping the distress, are not paid, then not earlier than the sixth day after the making of the distress, unless the accused consents in writing to an earlier sale, to sell the goods and pay the proceeds of the distress to the Clerk of the Magistrates' Court and if [no] [insufficient] distress can be found, to certify the same to that Magistrates' Court.

Justice of the Peace
[By order of the Court,
Clerk of the Court]

3. Attendance centre order: non-payment of fines (Form 3B in the Magistrates' Courts (Children and Young Persons) Rules 1988)

JUVENILE COURT (Code)

Date:

Defaulter: *Age:* *years*

Address:

Offence: *(Short particulars and Statute)*

Fine..................		The defaulter was on (date) adjudged to pay the total sum set out in the margin hereof
Compensation		[forthwith] [or (here see effect of order)] and has made default in payment of [the whole] [the balance set out in the margin.]
Costs.................		
Total................		
Part payments		
Balance...........		

Decision: The defaulter shall attend at the attendance centre on (*date*) at (*time*) and, subsequently, at such times as shall be fixed by the officer in charge of that centre, until the accused has completed a period of attendance of hours unless the outstanding sum is sooner paid (but see *Note 2* below).

Justice of the Peace.
[or By order of the Court
Clerk of the Court]

Note 1: The present address of the attendance centre specified above is:

Note 2: Under section 17(13) of the Criminal Justice Act 1982 the period of attendance may be reduced proportionately by payment of part of the outstanding sum.

4. Warrant of commitment on occasion of conviction (Form 51)

MAGISTRATES' COURT (Code)

Date:

Accused: *Age:* *years*

Address:

Offence: *(short particulars and statute)*

Ordered to pay: £ *fine*

£ *compensation*

£ *costs*

[Imprisonment] [detention] in default of payment:

To take effect forthwith because: *(state reason)*

*[This court is of the opinion that no method of dealing with the accused in respect of his default other than to order his detention is appropriate because (*state reason*)].

Direction: You, [the constables of Police Force] [the authorised persons for] [ ] are hereby required to convey the accused to [prison] [detention centre] [youth custody centre] and there deliver the accused to the Governor thereof, together with this warrant; and you, the Governor to receive into your custody and keep the accused for that period [to commence at the end of the term of [imprisonment] [detention] [youth custody] (*give particulars*)] unless the amount remaining due be sooner paid.

Justice of the Peace
[or By order of the Court
Clerk of the Court]

*Delete if the accused appears to have attained the age of 21 years.

5. Warrant of commitment on occasion subsequent to conviction (Form 52)

MAGISTRATES' COURT (Code)

Date:

Accused:

Addressed:

[Convicted on] [Unpaid fixed penalty registered for enforcement as a fine on]:

by the	[*Magistrates' Court*]
	[*Crown Court at*]
Offence:	*(short particulars and statute)*
Amount outstanding when [imprisonment] [detention] imposed:	£
[Imprisonment] [detention in] default of payment	*days*
Imposed on:	
by the:	[*Magistrates' Court*]

*[This court is satisfied that the default is due to the accused's wilful refusal or culpable neglect and has considered or tried all other methods of enforcing payment, namely—

(a) the making of a money payment supervision order;

(b) the making of an attachment of earnings order;

(c) the issue of a distress warrant;

(d) an application to the High Court or county court for remedies available in those courts;

(e) in the case of an offender under 21 years of age, the making of an attendance centre order.

and it appears to the court that all these methods are inappropriate or unsuccessful.] [The said offence is punishable with imprisonment and the accused appears to this court to have sufficient means to pay the amount remaining due] [the accused is already serving a term of imprisonment].

† [This court is of the opinion that no method of dealing with the accused in respect of his default other than to order his detention is appropriate because (*state reason*)].

†† [This court is satisfied that it is undesirable/impracticable to place the accused under supervision because (*state grounds*)]

Amount remaining due: £

Period to be served: *days*

Direction: You, [the Constables of Police Force] [the authorised persons for] [ ] are hereby required to convey the accused to [prison] [detention centre] [youth custody centre] and there deliver the accused to the Governor thereof, together with this warrant; and you, the Governor to receive into your custody and keep the accused for the said period of [to commence at the end of the term of [imprisonment] [detention] [youth custody] (*give particulars*)] unless the amount remaining due be sooner paid.

Justice of the Peace
[or by order of the Court
Clerk of the Court]

* Delete if a term of imprisonment has been fixed on a previous occasion.
† Delete if the accused appears to have attained the age of 21 years.
†† Delete if the accused appears to have attained the age of 21 years or has been placed under supervision.

6. Summons to fine defaulter (Form 53)

magistrates' court (Code)

Date:

To the accused:

Address:

Convicted on:

by the: [Magistrates' Court]
[Crown Court at]

Offence:	*(short particulars and statute)*	
Ordered to pay:	£	fine
	£	compensation
	£	costs
Total:	£	
Payments made:	£	
Amount still outstanding:	£	

You have failed to pay the amount shown above as still outstanding.

You are therefore hereby summoned to appear before the Magistrates' court sitting at on at unless the above amount has been paid in full beforehand, for inquiry to be made as to your means.

Justice of the Peace
[Justices' Clerk]

Note: The purpose of the inquiry as to your means is to enable the Court to decide whether or not to commit you to prison for default in payment. If you do not pay the outstanding amount in full and fail to appear in person in answer to this summons, you will render yourself liable to arrest without further notice.

7. Warrant for arrest of fine defaulter (Form 54)

MAGISTRATES' COURT (Code)

Date:

Accused:

Address:

Date penalty imposed:

by the: [Magistrates' Court]

[Crown Court at]

Total amount still outstanding: £

Direction: You [the Constables of Police Force] [the authorised persons for] [ ] are hereby required to arrest the accused and bring him before the Magistrates' Court at immediately.

**Bail* On arrest the accused shall be released on bail on entering into a recognizance in the sum of £ for the accused's appearance before the last mentioned Magistrates' Court at m. on unless the amount outstanding be sooner paid.

Justice of the Peace

* Delete if bail is not allowed and amend as appropriate where sureties are required or conditions imposed.

8. Warrant for detention in police cells, etc (Form 57)

MAGISTRATES' COURT (Code)

Date:

Accused: *Age:* *years*

Address:

Convicted on:

by the: [Magistrates' Court]

[Crown Court at]

Offence: (short particulars and statute)

Amount outstanding when imprisonment imposed: £

Imprisonment in default of payment: days

Imposed on:

by the: [Magistrates' Court]

[Crown Court at]

[(*Delete if a term of imprisonment has been fixed on a previous occasion*) [This court has considered or tried

all other methods of enforcing payment and it appears to this court that they are inappropriate or unsuccessful]
[The said offence is punishable with imprisonment and the accused appears to this court to have sufficient means to pay the amount remaining due]
[The accused is already serving a term of imprisonment]]
[(*Delete if the accused appears to have attained the age of 21 years*) This court is of the opinion that no method of dealing with the accused in respect of his default other than a sentence of imprisonment is appropriate because (*state reason*)]
[(*Delete if the accused appears to have attained the age of 21 years or has been placed under supervision*) This court is satisfied that it is undesirable/impracticable to place the accused under supervision because (*state grounds*)]

Amount remaining due: £

Period to be served: days

Directions: You [the Constables of Police Force] [the authorised persons for] [] are hereby required to convey the accused to (name of place) and there deliver the accused to the Police Officer in charge together with this warrant: and you the Police Officer in charge to receive into your custody and keep the accused for the said period of days unless the amount remaining due be sooner paid.

Justice of the Peace
[By order of the Court,
Clerk of the Court]

9. Warrant for detention in police station (Form 58)

MAGISTRATES' COURT (Code)

Date:

Accused: *Age:* *years*

Address:

Offence: *(short particulars and statute)*

Convicted on:

by the: Magistrates' Court

Ordered to pay: £ (*Total of fine, compensation and costs*)

Amount still outstanding: £

Direction: The accused having made default in payment of the amount shown above as still outstanding:

You the constables of Police Force are required to arrest the accused, unless the amount outstanding be sooner paid, and convey the accused to a police station and you the officer in charge of that station to detain the accused there until 8am on the day following that on which the accused is arrested between midnight and 8am until 8am on the day on which the accused is arrested provided that you the officer in charge of the police station may release the accused at any time between 4am and 8am if you think it expedient to do so in order to enable the accused to go to work or for any other reason appearing to you to be sufficient.

Justice of the Peace
[By order of the Court,
Clerk of the Court]

10. Transfer of fine order (Form 59)

MAGISTRATES' COURT (Code)

Date:

Accused: *Age:* *years*

Address:

Convicted on:

by the: [Magistrates' Court]

[Crown Court at]

Total amount ordered to pay: £ (*including fines, costs and compensation*)

Terms of payment:

Amount still outstanding: £

[Imprisonment fixed by the Crown Court in default of payment: (Applies to Crown Court fines only) days]

Order: This court being the court required to enforce payment of the amount shown above as still outstanding and it appears that the accused is residing at in the petty sessions area of (name area) a transfer of fine order is hereby made under section 89 of the Magistrates' Courts Act 1980 transferring to a magistrates' court acting for that petty sessions area to the clerk of that court, all the functions under Part II of that Act in respect of the amount shown above as still outstanding.

Justice of the Peace
[Justices' Clerk]

This order should be accompanied by a statement of the offence and of the steps, if any, taken to recover the sum together with any other available information which the clerk making the order thinks is likely to assist the receiving court. Names and addresses of persons to whom costs and compensation are payable, with details of amounts, must be included.

11. Transfer of fine order to Scotland or Northern Ireland (Form 60)

MAGISTRATES' COURT (Code)

Date:

Accused: *Age:* *years*

Address:

Convicted on:

by the: [Magistrates' Court]

[Crown Court at]

Total amount ordered to pay: £ *(including fines, costs and compensation)*

Terms of payment:

Amount still outstanding: £

[Imprisonment fixed by the Crown Court in default of payment: (Applies to Crown Court fines only) days]

Order: This court being the court required to enforce payment of the amount shown above as still outstanding and it appears that the accused is residing at within the jurisdiction of the court of summary jurisdiction in Scotland or Northern Ireland named below a transfer of fine order is hereby made under section 90 of the Magistrates' Courts Act 1980 transferring to the court of summary jurisdiction at (*state name and address of court*) the enforcement of payment of the amount shown above as still outstanding.

Justice of the Peace
[By order of the Court,
Clerk of the Court]

This order should be accompanied by a statement of the offence and of the steps, if any, taken to recover the sum together with any other available information which the clerk making the order thinks is likely to assist the receiving court. Names and addresses of persons to whom costs and compensation are payable, with details of amounts, must be included.

12. Notice of transfer of fine order (Form 61)

Date:

To the accused:

Address:

On (date) at [Magistrates' Court] [the Crown Court at] [a court of summary jurisdiction in [Scotland] [Northern Ireland], namely] you were ordered to pay the following amounts:

Fine: £

Compensation: £

Costs: £

Amounts still outstanding: £

Notice: YOU ARE HEREBY GIVEN NOTICE that in consequence of a transfer of fine order made on (*date*) the enforcement of payment of the amount still outstanding has now become a matter for the Magistrates' Court.

Payment of the amount outstanding should now be made to the court named below [immediately] [before (*date*)].

If you are unable to pay you should at once make an application for [further] time to be granted by letter addressed to me setting out fully the grounds of your application.

Payment must be made personally at the address shown below on (days) between (time) and (time) or—

By post to the address shown below. Crossed cheques and postal orders should be made payable to the "Justices' Clerk". Cash should not be sent in unregistered envelopes. Any communications sent by post must be properly stamped.

Payment to: The Justices Clerk,
Telephone no:

Justices' Clerk

13. Notice of fine supervision order (Form 62)

MAGISTRATES' COURT (Code)

Date:

To the Accused:

Address:

On (date) at [Magistrates' Court] [the Crown Court at] you were ordered to pay the following amounts:

Fine	£
Compensation:	£
Costs	£
Amount still outstanding:	£
Notice:	You are hereby given notice that you were [today] [on (*date*)] by order of this Court, placed under the supervision of (*name and address*) until you have paid the amount shown above as still outstanding or a further order be made.
	[Payment is to be made by weekly/monthly instalments of £ , the first instalment to be paid immediately.]
	Justices' Clerk

14. Authority for clerk of magistrates' court to enforce payment of fine in High Court or county court (Form 63)

MAGISTRATES' COURT (Code)

Date:	
Accused:	
Address:	
[Convicted on]	*[Unpaid fixed penalty registered for enforcement as a fine on]:*
by the:	[Magistrates' Court] [Crown Court at]
Offence:	*(short particulars and statute)*
Ordered to pay:	£ fine
	£ compensation
	£ costs
	[This court being the court required under section 32(1) of the Powers of Criminal Courts Act 1973 to enforce payment of the sum shown above:
	And] The accused having made default in payment of the amount remaining due:
Amount remaining due:	£

This court having inquired into the accused's means hereby authorises the Clerk of the Court to take the undermentioned proceedings in the [High Court] [County Court] for the recovery of the amount remaining due.

Nature of proceedings:

Justice of the Peace.

Fixed penalties

[All forms are in the Magistrates' Courts (Forms) Rules 1981.]

15. Notification to fixed penalty clerk of registration of unpaid fixed penalty as a fine (Form 158)

To: The Fixed Penalty Clerk,

NOTIFICATION OF REGISTRATION

Fixed Penalty Notice No: Date Issued:

Time/Place Issued (as appropriate)

Vehicle Registration No: Driver Licence No:

Offence:

Fixed Penalty £ Sum payable in default £

Defaulter's name:

Defaulter's address:

I hereby give notice that the above-mentioned sum payable in default of payment of a fixed penalty has been registered for enforcement as a fine against the defaulter named.

Justices' Clerk

16. Notice to defaulter of registration of unpaid fixed penalty as a fine (Form 159)

MAGISTRATES' COURT (Code)

Date:

To of

Notice to Owner/Hirer No:
Fixed Penalty Notice No: Date issued:

Time/Place Issued (as appropriate)

Vehicle Registration No: *Driver's Licence No:

Offence:

You are hereby given notice that the sum of £ equal to the fixed penalty payable under the notice noted above plus one half of that fixed penalty, has been registered in this Court under the authority given by sections [30(3)][32(2)] and 36(6) of the Transport Act 1982*. Payment of this outstanding amount is now due and should be made either in person at the address shown below on between or sent by post to the address shown below. Cheques and postal orders should be crossed and made payable to the Justices' Clerk. Cash should not be sent in unregistered envelopes. Any communication sent by post must be properly stamped. The address of the court is:

The Magistrates' Court
(address)

Correspondence should be address to the Justices' Clerk.

If you do not now pay the sum due, a distress warrant (which will permit the seizure and sale of goods to the value of the outstanding sum) may be issued against you or you may be required to appear or be arrested and brought before the court for an inquiry into your means. Application for further time for payment may be made in writing or in person to the Justices' Clerk at the above address stating the grounds of the application.

Justices' Clerk

Note:—This Notice should be sent/brought with any payment, enquiry or application.

* Now the Road Traffic Offenders Act 1988.

17. Statutory declaration (driver present) (Form 160)

I (name) of sincerely declare that:

*A I was not the person to whom the fixed penalty notice, number , was issued on , in respect of vehicle, registration mark , and for which the sum payable in default was registered as a fine on by Magistrates' Court.

*B With reference to the fixed penalty notice number issued on , in respect of vehicle, registration mark , and for which the sum payable in default was registered as a fine on , by Magistrates' Court, on I requested a hearing in the manner specified in the fixed penalty notice.

And I make this solemn declaration conscientiously believing the same to be true, and by virtue of the provisions of the Statutory Declarations Act 1835.

Dated the (date)

(signature of person making the declaration)

Declared before me (signature of Justice of the Peace)

Name of Justice (in block letters)

*delete as applicable

Note: Any person who knowingly and wilfully makes a statutory declaration which is false in a material particular is guilty of an offence and liable on conviction to a term of imprisonment for a period of up to 2 years or to a fine or to both (section 5 of the Perjury Act 1911).

18. Statutory declaration (driver not present) (Form 161)

I (name) of (address) do solemnly and sincerely declare that:—

*A with reference to the fixed penalty notice/notice to owner/notice to hirer number , issued on , in respect of vehicle, registration mark , and for which the sum payable in default was registered as a fine on , by Magistrates' Court, I did not know of the fixed penalty concerned or of any fixed penalty notice/notice to owner/notice to hirer relating to that penalty until I received notice of registration.

*B I was not the owner/hirer of the vehicle, registration mark , at the time of the alleged offence on , of which particulars are given in notice to owner/notice to hirer number , and for which the sum payable in default was registered as a fine on , by Magistrates' Court and have reasonable excuse for failing to comply with the requirements of that notice to owner/notice to hirer, namely, that

*C With reference to the notice to owner/notice to hirer number , issued on , in respect of vehicle, registration mark , and for which the sum payable in default was registered as a fine on , by Magistrates' Court on I requested a hearing in the manner specified by the notice to owner/notice to hirer.

And I make this solemn declaration conscientiously believing the same to be true, and by virtue of the provisions of the Statutory Declarations Act 1835.

Dated the (date)

(signature of person making the declaration)

Declared before me (signature of Justice of the Peace)

Name of Justice (in block letters)

*delete as applicable

Note: Any person who knowingly and wilfully makes a statutory declaration which is false in a material particular is guilty of an offence and liable on conviction to a term of imprisonment for a period of up to 2 years or to a fine or to both (section 5 of the Perjury Act 1911).

Enforcement of maintenance orders

[All forms are in the Magistrates' Courts (Maintenance Order Act 1958) Rules 1959 unless otherwise indicated.]

19. Extract from register proving proceedings of a magistrates' court (Form 154 in the Magistrates' Courts (Forms) Rules 1981)

In the [county of Petty Sessional Division of].

Memorandum of a conviction [or order (or other proceeding) entered in the Register of the Magistrates' Court sitting at , the day of , 19

Name of informant or of complaint	*Name of defendant Age, if known*	*Nature of offence or matter of complaint*	*Date of offence or matter of complaint*	*Plea of consent to order*	*Minute of adjudication*	*Time allowed for payment and instalments*

I certify the above extract to be a true copy.

Clerk of the said Magistrates' Court.

Dated the day of , 19

20. Certificate of clerk of magistrates' court of non-payment of sums adjudged (Form 146 in the Magistrates' Courts (Forms) Rules 1981)

MAGISTRATES' COURT (Code)

Date

I hereby certify that the payments due to me on behalf of from under an order made by the Magistrates' Court on (*date*) under the (State the Act under which the order was made) have not been made to me in full and there is now in arrear the sum of £ in respect of [periodical payments] [instalments] due up to and including (*date*).

Justices' Clerk

21. Declaration as to non-payment of sums adjudged (Form 147 Magistrates' Courts (Forms) Rules 1981)

I, of , do solemnly and sincerely declare that the payments due to me from under an order made by the Magistrates' Court sitting at , on the day of 19 , under (*state the Act under which the order was made*) have not been made to me in full, and that there is now in arrear the sum of [in respect of periodical payments [or instalments] due up to and including the day of , 19].

And I make this solemn declaration, conscientiously believing the same to be true, by virtue of the provisions of the Statutory Declarations Act 1935.

(Signed)

Declared at the day of , 19 before me.

Justice of the Peace for the [county] of
(Or other description)

22. Warrant of commitment for the enforcement of maintenance order or order enforceable as magistrates' court maintenance order for use in case of immediate issue (Form 18)

In the county of Petty Sessional Division of

To each and all of the Constables of and to the Governor of Her Majesty's prison at (or the Police Officer in charge of).

Whereas on a complaint made by of, that of (hereinafter called the defendant) had made default in payment of the sums ordered to be paid by (*insert particulars of maintenance order*) it was proved to the Magistrates' Court sitting at , that the defendant did owe to of the sum of under the order and the sum of for costs thereunder.

And whereas the Court having inquired in the presence of the defendant whether the default was due to his wilful refusal or culpable neglect is not of the opinion that it was not so due.

And whereas [the Court is of opinion that it is inappropriate to make an attachment of earnings order] [there is no power to make an attachment of earnings order].

It is ordered, the defendant not being absent, that he be committed to prison (or detained in police custody) for (*state period*) unless he sooner pays the said sums due from him as aforesaid [together with the costs of enforcement] as set out below.

You the said Constables are hereby required to take the defendant and convey him to the Governor of her Majesty's prison (or the Police Officer in charge of) at and you the said Governor (or Police Officer) to receive the defendant into your custody and keep him for (*state period*) from his arrest under this order or until he be sooner discharged in due course of law.

Dated the day of 19

Justice of the Peace for the (county) first above mentioned

or By order of the court

Clerk of the Magistrates' Court sitting at

Amount found due ....£

Deductions in respect of Income Tax ....£

Net amount ....£

Enforcement costs payable ....£

Total sum payable by defendant ....£

Endorsement of payments

Date of Receipt £ p *Signature*

23. Warrant of commitment for enforcement of maintenance order or order enforceable as magistrates' court maintenance order for use where issue has been postponed (Form 19)

In the county of Petty Sessional Division of

To each and all of the Constables of and to the Governor of Her Majesty's prison at (or the Police Officer in charge of).

Whereas on a complaint made by of , that of (hereinafter called the defendant) has made default in payment of the sums ordered to be paid by (*insert particulars of maintenance order*) it was proved to the Magistrates' Court sitting at , that the defendant did owe to of for costs thereunder.

And whereas the Court having inquired in the presence of the defendant whether the default was due to his wilful refusal or culpable neglect is not of the opinion that it was not so due.

And whereas [the Court is of opinion that it is inappropriate to make an attachment of earnings order] [there was no power to make an attachment of earnings order].

And whereas the Court, the defendant not being absent, on the day of , 19 , fixed a term of imprisonment (*insert term*) and postponed issue of the warrant of commitment (*insert term of postponement unless there has been a further postponement*).

[And whereas on the application of the defendant the Court on the day of 19 further postponed the issue of the warrant (*insert terms of further postponement*)]

[And whereas on the application of the defendant the warrant having been executed the Court cancelled the warrant of commitment but fixed a further term of imprisonment (*insert term*) and postponed issue of the further warrant of commitment (*insert terms of postponement*):]

And whereas under the said terms of postponement the said warrant fell to be issued and the Clerk of the Court gave notice to the defendant that he might make an application to the Court requesting that the warrant should not be issued.

[And whereas no such application was received by the Clerk within the prescribed period.]

[And whereas such an application was made and considered by [me] (the Court).]

[And whereas by reason of part payment the said sums remaining due from the defendant as aforesaid are reduced in amount to]

It is ordered that the defendant be committed to prison [or detained in police custody] for (*state period*) unless he sooner pays the said sums [remaining] due from him as aforesaid (together with the costs of enforcement as set out below.

You the said Constables are hereby required to take the defendant and convey him to the Governor of Her Majesty's prison [or the Police Officer in charge of] and you the said Governor [or Police Officer], to receive the defendant into your custody and keep him for (*state period*) from his arrest under this order or until he be sooner discharged in due course of law.

Dated the day of , 19

Justice of the Peace for the (county) first above mentioned
or By order of the court

Clerk of the Magistrates' Court sitting at

Amount found due ....£
Deductions in respect of Income Tax ....£
Net amount...£
Paid ....£
Net amount remaining due ....£
Enforcement costs payable.......................................£
Total sum payable by defendant ....£

Endorsement of payments

Date of Receipt	£	p	*Signature*

24. Notice that warrant of commitment falls to be issued (Form 15)

In the (county of Petty Sessional Division of)

Before the Magistrates' Court sitting at

To of

PLEASE READ THIS NOTICE CAREFULLY

On the day of , 19 , this Court postponed the issue of a warrant of commitment in your case for the enforcement of (*insert particulars of maintenance order*) (*insert the terms of postponement*)].

You have failed to comply with these terms of postponement and the warrant committing you to prison for a term of now falls to be issued unless you pay under the maintenance order [the sum] [the net sum, after making deductions in respect of income tax], of

If you consider that there are grounds for not issuing the warrant you may make an application to the Court on the attached form requesting that the warrant shall not be issued and stating those grounds.

If no such application is received by me on or before the day of

19 and you fail to pay the sum referred to above the warrant will be issued.

If such an application is received by me on or before the day of 19 it will be considered by a justice who may either refer it to the Court for further consideration or dismiss the application and issue the warrant forthwith.

Dated the day of , 19

Clerk of the Magistrates' Court sitting at

25. Application requesting that warrant should not be issued (Form 16)

To the Magistrates' Court sitting at

I of have received the notice sent to me by the Clerk of the Court and dated the day of 19

I hereby request that the warrant of commitment shall not be issued. The grounds of my request are as follows:

Dated the day of 19

(Signed)

Note: This application should be delivered or sent by post to the Clerk of the Court (*insert address*).

26. Application requesting that warrant should be cancelled (Form 17)

To the Magistrates' Court sitting at

I, , hereby request that the warrant of commitment under which I am for the time being imprisoned (or otherwise detained) should be cancelled. The grounds of my request are as follows:

Dated the day of 19

(Signed)

27. [Not reproduced]

28. Notice that payments have become payable through the clerk of a magistrates' court (Form 8)

MAGISTRATES' COURT

Date:

To:

Address:

You are hereby given notice that the sums payable by you under (*insert particulars of maintenance order*) made on the day of 19 by the [High Court] [County Court] [Court of Session] [High Court in Northern Ireland] and registered in this Court under Part I of the Maintenance Orders Act 1958, have under an order of this Court dated the day of 19 , become payable through [me] [the Clerk of the Magistrates' Court sitting at].

Payments under the order (including payments in respect of any sums due at the date of the receipt by you of this notice should henceforth be sent to the Clerk of the Magistrates' Court at (state address).

Justices' Clerk

29. Certificate of clerk of magistrates' court that no process for enforcement remains in force and no proceedings for variations are pending (Form 3)

I hereby certify that at the date of this certificate no process remains in force for the enforcement and no proceedings are pending in the Magistrates' Court for the variation of (*insert particulars of maintenance order*) made on the day of 19 by the [High Court] [County Court] [Court of Session] [High Court in Northern Ireland] the payments whereunder are at present required to be made through me.

Dated the day of 19

Clerk of the Magistrates' Court sitting at

30. Notice of cancellation of registration of a High Court or county court order (Form 10)

MAGISTRATES' COURT

Date:

To:

Address:

You are hereby given notice that the registration in this Court under Part I of the Maintenance Orders Act 1958, of (*insert particulars of maintenance order*) made on the day of 19 by the [High Court] [County Court] [Court of Session] [High Court in Northern Ireland] has been cancelled.

Sums payable by you under the said order have by reason of the cancellation of the registration of the said order ceased to be payable through (*state clerk of the Magistrates' Court through whom payments have hitherto been required to be made*).

Payments under the order (including payments in respect of any sum due on the date of the receipt by you of this notice) should henceforth be paid to (*state name and address of person entitled to payments under this order*)

Justices' Clerk

31. Certificate of arrears (Form 3 in the Maintenance Orders Act 1950 (Summary Jurisdiction) Rules 1950)

I hereby certify that the arrears due at the date of this certificate (*insert particulars of maintenance order*) made on the day of 19 by the Magistrates' Court sitting at (*address*), the payments whereunder are at present required to be made to [or through] me, amount to £

Dated the day of 19.

Collecting Officer of the Magistrates' Court sitting at (*address*).

32. Notice to person liable to make payments that sums payable under a maintenance order made by a court of summary jurisdiction in England have ceased to be payable to or through an officer or person (Form 2 in the Maintenance Orders Act 1950 (Summary Jurisdiction) Rules 1950)

In the (county of Petty Sessional Division of)
Magistrates' Court sitting at (*address*)

To of

You are hereby given notice that the sums payable by you under (*insert particulars of maintenance order*) made on the day of 19 by this court have, by reason of the registration of the said order in (*state court in Scotland or Northern Ireland in which order is registered*) ceased to be payable through (or to) (*state officer or person through or to whom payments have hitherto been required to be made*).

Payments under the order (including payments in respect of any sums due at the date of the receipt by you of this notice) should henceforth be paid to (*state name and address of the person entitled to payments under the order*) [unless you receive, or have meanwhile received, notice from the clerk of the said court in Northern Ireland that they are to be paid to any other person].

Dated the day of 19

Clerk (and collecting officer) of the Magistrates' Court at (*address*).

33. Certificate of clerk of magistrates' court that no process for enforcement remains in force (Form 2)

(MOA 1958, s 2(4)(c))

I hereby certify that at the date of this certificate no process remains in force for the enforcement of (*insert particulars of maintenance order*) made on day of 19 by the Magistrates' Court sitting at , the payments whereunder are at present required to be made to me.

Dated the day of 19

Clerk of the Magistrates' Court sitting at

34. Certificate of clerk of magistrates' court that copy of maintenance order is a true copy sent for registration (Form 7)

(MOA 1958, s 2(4)(c))

I hereby certify that this is a true copy of (*insert particulars of maintenance order*) and that it is sent to in accordance with the provisions of paragraph (c) of subsection (4) of section two of the Maintenance Orders Act 1958, and of Rule 3 to the Magistrates' Courts (Maintenance Orders Act 1958) Rules 1959.

Dated the day of 19

Clerk of the Magistrates' Court sitting at

35. Notice that payments have ceased to be payable through the clerk of the magistrates' court (Form 9)

(MOA 1958, s 2(5); MOA 1950, s 19(4))

MAGISTRATES' COURT (Code)

Date:

To:

Address:

You are hereby given notice that the sums payable by you under (*insert particulars of maintenance order*) made on the day of 19 by [this Court] (*state court in Scotland or Northern Ireland which made the order*) and registered in this Court (under Part II of the Maintenance Orders Act 1950) have by reason of the registration of the said order in the High Court ceased to be payable to (*state clerk of magistrates' court to whom payments have hitherto been required to be made*).

Payments under the order (including payments in respect of any sums due at the date of the receipt by you of this notice) should henceforth be paid to (state name and address of the persons entitled to payments under this order).

Justices' Clerk

36. Notice to person liable to make payments that sums payable under a maintenance order registered in a court of summary jurisdiction in England have become payable through collecting officer (Form 1 in the Maintenance Orders Act 1950 (Summary Jurisdiction) Rules 1950)

(MOA 1958, s 19(4))

MAGISTRATES' COURT (Code)

In the (county of Petty Sessional Division of)

Court of Summary Jurisdiction sitting at

To of

You are hereby given notice that the sums payable by you under (insert particulars of maintenance order) made on the day of 19 by (*state court in Scotland or Northern Ireland which made the order*) and registered in this Court under Part II of the Maintenance Orders Act 1950, have, under an order of this Court dated the day of 19 become payable through (or to) the Collecting Officer of this Court (or the Court of Summary Jurisdiction sitting at).

Payments under the order (including payments in respect of any sums due at the date of the receipt by you of this notice) should henceforth be sent to me (or to the said Collecting Officer) at (*state address*).

Dated the day of 19

Justices' Clerk

Attachment of earnings

[All forms are in the Magistrates' Courts (Attachment of Earnings) Rules 1971.]

37. Attachment of earnings order: maintenance (Form 1)

PRIORITY

In the (County of Petty Sessional Division of)

Before the Magistrates' Court sitting at

To of of who works at as a (Works No) is required to make payments of £ a [week] under a maintenance order made on by the (*insert court*). An application has been made for an attachment of earnings order to secure the payments and it appears that earnings are payable by you to him.

You are ordered to make out of those earnings periodical deductions in accordance with Schedule 3 to the Attachment of Earnings Act 1971. For the purpose of calculating the deductions the normal deduction rate shall be £ a [week] and the protected earnings rate shall be £ a [week].

And you are ordered to pay the sums deducted to the Clerk of [this Court] [the Magistrates' Court sitting at (whose address is)] as and when the deductions are made.

Dated

Justice of the Peace for the [county] aforesaid.
[or By order of the Court, Clerk of the Court.]

Note: A copy of an explanatory booklet [is enclosed] [may be obtained from the Clerk of the Court].

Indorsement on copy sent to debtor

This is a copy of an attachment of earnings order directed to your employer. If you leave this employment or become employed or re-employed, you must notify the Court in writing within seven days, giving particulars of your earnings and anticipated earnings from any new employment.

Failure to do so may render you liable to a fine.

38. Attachment of earnings order: lump sum (Form 2)

PRIORITY

In the (County of Petty Sessional Division of)

Before the Magistrates' Court sitting at

To of of who works at as a (Works No) is required to pay a sum to which section 1(3)(b) or (c) of the Attachment of Earnings Act 1971 applies and it appears that earnings are payable by you to him.

You are ordered to make out of those earnings periodical deductions in accordance with Schedule 3 to the Attachment of Earnings Act 1971 until the amount of that sum remaining unpaid, namely £ , [on the date of this variation of an earlier order], has been deducted. For the purposes of calculating the deductions the normal deduction rate shall be £ a [week], and the protected earnings rate shall be £ a [week].

And you are ordered to pay the sums deducted to the Clerk of this Court as an when the deductions are made.

Dated

Justice of the Peace for the [county] aforesaid.
[or By order of the Court, Clerk of the Court.]

Note: A copy of an explanatory booklet [is enclosed] [may be obtained from the Clerk of the Court].

Indorsement on copy sent to debtor

This is a copy of an attachment of earnings order directed to your employer. If you leave this employment or become employed or re-employed, you must notify the Court in writing within seven days, giving particulars of your earnings and anticipated earnings from any new employment.

Failure to do so may render you liable to a fine.

39. Temporary variation order (Form 3)

In the (County of Petty Sessional Division of)

To of

An attachment of earnings order made by the Magistrates' Court sitting at in respect of of (hereinafter called the defendant) who works at as a (Works No) has been served on you and the defendant has applied for a temporary variation in the order.

You are ordered to make deductions under that order as if it specified as in the protected earnings rate an increased rate of £ a [week].

This variation shall remain in force for a period of [four] weeks.

Dated

Justice of the Peace for the [county] aforesaid.
[or Justices' Clerk.]

Note: On the expiry of this temporary variation order, deductions should be made in accordance with the attachment of earnings order.

Civil debt

[All forms are in the Magistrates' Courts (Forms) Rules 1981.]

40. Complaint: civil debt (Form 104)

MAGISTRATES' COURT (Code)

Date:

Defendant:

Address:

Matter of complaint: *(State grounds of complaint)*

The complaint of:

Address: Telephone no: who [upon oath] states that the defendant was responsible for the matter of complaint of which particulars are given above and claims from the defendant the following sum which is recoverable summarily as a civil debt:

Debt: £

Taken [and sworn] before me

Justice of the Peace
[Justices' Clerk]

41. Summons to defendant: civil debt (Form 105)

MAGISTRATES' COURT (Code)

Date:

To the defendant:

of:

YOU ARE HEREBY SUMMONED to appear, unless the sum specified below be sooner paid, before the Magistrates' Court sitting at on (*date*) at m to answer to the following complaint:

Matter of complaint: *(State grounds of complaint)*

and that you have failed to pay the following sums which are recoverable summarily as a civil debt:

Debt: £

Costs: £

Complainant:

Address:

Date of complaint:

Justice of the Peace
[Justices' Clerk]

42. Order: civil debt (Form 106)

MAGISTRATES' COURT (Code)

Date:

Defendant:

Address:

Complainant: On the complaint of:

Address:

Matter of complaint: *(State grounds of complaint)*

it is adjudged that the complaint is true and it is ordered:

Order: that the defendant pay to the complainant the sum of [being an amount recoverable summarily as a civil debt and] for costs.

Payment is to be made [by weekly/monthly instalments of the first instalment to be paid] [immediately] [not later than *(date)*].

[And it is ordered that in default of payment the sum due be levied by distress and sale of the goods of the defendant.]

Justice of the Peace
[By order of the Court, Clerk of the Court]

43. Distress warrant: civil debt (Form 109)

MAGISTRATES' COURT (Code)

Date:

Debtor:

Address:

Amount ordered to be paid: £ being money recoverable summarily as a civil debt.

Costs: £

The debtor was on (date) at [Magistrates' Court] [the Crown Court at] ordered to pay the sums specified above [by weekly/monthly instalments of £ , the first instalment to be paid] [immediately] [by]

The debtor has been served with a copy of a minute of the order and default has been made in payment:

Total amount still outstanding: £

Direction: You [the constables of Police Force] [ ] are hereby required immediately to make distress of the money and goods of the accused (except the clothing and bedding of the accused and the accused's family, and to the value of fifty pounds, the tools and implements of the accused's trade); and if the amount shown above as still outstanding, together with the costs and charges of taking and keeping the distress, are not paid, then not earlier than the sixth day after the making of the distress, unless the accused consents in writing to an earlier sale, to sell the goods and pay the proceeds of the distress to the Clerk of the Magistrates' Court and if [no] [insufficient] distress can be found to certify the same to that Magistrates' Court.

Justice of the Peace
[By order of the Court, Clerk of the Court]

44. Complaint to enforce civil debt order (Form 107)

MAGISTRATES' COURT (Code)

Date:

Debtor:

Address:

The complaint of:

Address:

Telephone no: who [upon oath] states that on (*date*) the debtor was ordered by the [Magistrates' Court] [Crown Court at] to pay the complainant the following sum[s]:

Sum[s] ordered to be paid: £

Costs: £ to be paid

and the debtor has made default in payment.

Amount paid: £

Total amount outstanding: £

Amount of default: £

Taken [and sworn] before me

Justice of the Peace
[Justices' Clerk]

45. Judgment summons (Form 108)

MAGISTRATES' COURT (Code)

Date:

To:

of:

Matter of complaint: that on (date) at [Magistrates' Court] [the Crown Court at] you were ordered to pay to the complainant the sum shown below and that you have made default in payment of that sum.

Complainant:

of:

Amount ordered to be paid: £

Costs: £

Amount paid: £

Amount still outstanding: £

Amount of default: £

YOU ARE HEREBY SUMMONED to appear on (date) at m before the Magistrates' Court sitting at to answer to the above complaint and for inquiry to be made as to the means you have had since the order for payment was made to pay the sum or any instalment of it, and to show cause why you should not be committed to prison in accordance with section 96 of the Magistrates' Courts Act 1980, in default of payment.

Justice of the Peace
[Justices' Clerk]

46. Commitment: civil debt enforceable by imprisonment (Form 110)

MAGISTRATES' COURT (Code)

Date:

Debtor:

Address:

Was on (date) by the [Crown

[Magistrates'] Court at ordered to pay the sum[s] shown below:

£

£ costs

of which there is still outstanding the sum of

Amount still outstanding £

The court is satisfied that the debtor [has] [has had since the date of the above order] the means to pay the sum [now] due and [refuses or neglects] [has refused or neglected] to pay the sum.

[It appears that [no] [insufficient] distress could be found upon which the levy the sum due.]

Decision: that the debtor be [committed to prison] [detained in police custody] for:
unless the amount outstanding together with the costs are sooner paid.

Direction: You [the constables of Police Force] [ ] are hereby required to take the debtor and convey him to Prison] [ ] and there deliver the debtor to the [Governor] [Police officer in charge] thereof and you the [Governor] [Police officer in charge] to receive the debtor into your custody and keep the debtor for (*state period*) from the debtor's arrest under this order or until the debtor be sooner discharged in due course of law.

Justice of the Peace
[By order of the Court, Clerk of the Court]

47. Liability order prescribed form

Section 33 of the Child Support Act 1991 and regulation 29(1) of the Child Support (Collection and Enforcement) Regulations 1992

MAGISTRATES' COURT

Date:

Defendant:

Address:

On the complaint of the Secretary of State for Social Security that the sums specified below are due from the defendant under the Child Support Act 1991 and Part IV of the Child Support (Collection and Enforcement) Regulations 1992 and are outstanding, it is adjudged that the defendant is liable to pay the aggregate amount specified below.

Sum payable and outstanding	child support maintenance interest other periodical payments collected by virtue of section 30 of the Child Support Act 1991

Aggregate amount in respect of which the liability order is made:

Justice of the Peace

[*or* by order of the Court
Clerk of the Court]

48. Form of warrant of commitment

Section 40 of the Child Support Act 1991 and regulation 34(1) of the Child Support (Collection and Enforcement) Regulations 1992

MAGISTRATES' COURT

Date:

Liable Person:

Address:

A liability order ("the order") was made against the liable person by the [ ] Magistrates' Court on [ ] under section 33 of the Child Support Act 1991 ("the Act") in respect of an amount of [ ].

The court is satisfied–

(i) that the Secretary of State sought under section 35 of the Act to levy by distress the amount then outstanding in respect of which the order was made;

[and /or]

that the Secretary of State sought under section 36 of the Act to recover through the [ ] County Court, by means of [garnishee proceedings] or [a charging order], the amount then outstanding in respect of which the order was made;

(ii) that such an amount, or any portion of it, remains unpaid; and
(iii) having inquired in the liable person's presence as to his means and as to whether there has been [wilful refusal] or [culpable neglect] on his part, the court is of the opinion that there has been [wilful refusal] or [culpable neglect] on his part.

The decision of the court is that the liable person be [committed to prison] [detained] for [ ] unless the aggregate amount mentioned below in respect of which this warrant is made is sooner paid.*

This warrant is made in respect of–
Amount outstanding (including any interest, costs and charges):
Costs of commitment of the Secretary of State:

Aggregate amount:

And you *[name of the person or persons to whom the warrant is directed]* are hereby required to take the liable person and convey him to *[name of prison and place of detention]* and then deliver him to the [governor] [officer in charge] thereof; and you, the [governor] [officer in charge], to receive the liable person into your custody and keep him for *[period of imprisonment]* from the date of his arrest under this warrant or until he be sooner discharged in due course of law.

Justice of the Peace

[*or* by order of the Court
Clerk of the Court].

Note: The period of imprisonment will be reduced as provided by regulation 34(5) and (6) of the Child Support (Collection and Enforcement) Regulations 1992 if part-payment is made of the aggregate amount.

Community Charge/Council Tax

49. Warrant of commitment

Regulation 41 of the Community Charges (Administration and Enforcement) Regulations 1989

MAGISTRATES' COURT

Date:

Debtor:

Address:

A liability order ("the order") was made in respect of the debtor by the [ ] Magistrates' Court on [ ] under regulation 29 of the Community Charges (Administration and Enforcement) Regulations 1989 ("the Regulations").

The court is satisfied–

(i) that the [(name of charging authority)] ("the authority") sought under regulation 39 of the Regulations to levy by distress the amount then outstanding in respect of which the order was made of [ ], together with charges determined in accordance with Schedule 5 to the Regulations of [ ];

(ii) that no (or insufficient) goods of the debtor can be found by the authority on which to levy that amount; and

(iii) having inquired in the debtor's presence as to his means and as to whether the failure to pay which led to the order being made against him was due to his wilful refusal or culpable neglect, that it was due to such wilful refusal or culpable neglect.

The decision of the court is that the debtor be [committed to prison] [detained] for [ ] unless the aggregate amount mentioned below in respect of which this warrant is made is sooner paid.*

This warrant is made in respect of–

Amount outstanding (including charges) in respect of which the distress was sought:

Costs of commitment of the authority:

Aggregate amount:

And you *[(name of the person or persons to whom the warrant is directed)]* are hereby required to take the debtor and convey him to [*(name of prison and place of detention)]* and then deliver the debtor to the [governor] [officer in charge] thereof; and you, the [governor] [officer in charge], to receive the debtor into your custody and keep the debtor for *[(period of imprisonment)]* from the debtor's arrest under this warrant or until the debtor be sooner discharged in due course of law.

Justice of the Peace

[*or* by order of the Court
Clerk of the Court].

Note: The period of imprisonment will be reduced as provided by regulation 41(7)(b) of the Regulations if part payment is made of the aggregate amount.

50. Warrant of commitment

Regulation 47 of the Council Tax (Administration and Enforcement) Regulations 1992

MAGISTRATES' COURT

Date:

Defendant:

Address:

A liability order ("the order') was made in respect of the debtor by the [ ] Magistrates' Court on [ ] under regulation 34 of the Council Tax (Administration and Enforcement) Regulations 1992 ("the Regulations").

The court is satisfied–

(i) that the [*name of billing authority*] ("the authority") sought under regulation 45 of the Regulations to levy by distress the amount then outstanding in respect of which the order was made of [ ], together with charges determined in accordance with Schedule 5 to the Regulations of [ ];
(ii) that the authority has been unable to levy that amount by distress;
(iii) that the debtor has attained the age of 18 years; and
(iv) having inquired in the debtor's presence as to his means and as to whether the failure to pay which led to the application for a warrant of commitment is due to his wilful refusal or culpable neglect, that it was due to such wilful refusal or culpable neglect.

The decision of the court is that the debtor be [committed to prison] [detained] for [ ] unless the aggregate amount mentioned below in respect of which this warrant is made is sooner paid.*

This warrant is made in respect of–

Amount outstanding (including charges)
in respect of which the distress was sought:

Costs of commitment of the authority:

Aggregate amount:

And you [*name of the person or persons to whom the warrant is directed*] are hereby required to take the debtor and convey him to [*name of prison and place of detention*] and then deliver the debtor to the [governor] [officer in charge] thereof; and you, the [governor] [officer in charge], to receive the debtor into your custody and keep the debtor for *[period of imprisonment]* from the debtor's arrest under this warrant or until the debtor be sooner discharged in due course of law.

Justice of the Peace
[*or* by order of the Court
Clerk of the Court].

Note: The period of imprisonment will be reduced as provided by regulation 47(7)(b) of the Regulations if part payment is made of the aggregate amount.

Index